CW01394578

The
Philosopher's
Snack Pack

A selection of short and stimulating articles from

The ***Philosophers'***
Magazine

edited by

Julian Baggini and Jeremy Stangroom

First published in 1999 by
TPM (The Philosophers' Magazine)
21 Parkhurst Road
London
N22 8JQ
Tel: 020 8889 7041
Fax: 020 8643 1504
Email: editor@philosophers.co.uk
www.philosophers.co.uk

A catalogue record for this book is
available from the British Library

ISBN 0 9537611 0 X

Printed in Great Britain by
Bookcraft, Midsomer Norton, Somerset.

Snack selection

plus cartoons by Stamp

with grateful thanks to the many people who have helped make the first two years of The Philosophers' Magazine a success

Preface

Is it possible to have a "philosophical snack?" After all, isn't philosophy by its very nature something heavy, substantial, something that needs to be devoured slowly, chewed over and digested?

Trust a book on philosophy to start with some questions. What of the answers? Philosophers are a misunderstood bunch and if there's one thing that gets them going it is the idea that someone, somewhere, is misrepresenting their subject, making it out to be easy and "dip-in-to-able" when really it's a hard and complex slog. And well they might complain. It is true – philosophy is difficult, it is complex and it is a subject of great substance.

So how can you have a philosopher's snack pack?

The answer is simple: what's wrong with indulging in the odd tasting here and there before committing yourself to a full serving? This is essentially a book of appetisers, not full meals. If you find yourself stimulated by what you find, you can always go in deeper another time. Even the most ardent philosopher cannot go into the fine detail of subjects outside their specialisms. The choice is therefore simple: taste a little of many things or eat a lot of a few. There's a balance to be struck here, but I am sure the right balance leaves room for some "snacking" – just so along as snacking is not all you do.

Of course, it's also possible that you'll discover that, though you quite like a taste of philosophy, you don't think you could stomach too much of the stuff. In which case, you've had some fun, and as long as you don't go away with the idea that you now know all there is to know about philosophy, I can't see why anyone would object to your little indulgence.

So, tuck in, see what you fancy. Before deciding whether to sit at the gourmets' table, it's worth checking out whether you like what's on the menu.

Paradoxes
1: The Liar

Francis Moorcroft

Suppose someone said to you
> "What I am now saying is a lie."

Is what they said true or false? If what they said was true, then they are telling a lie, so it is false; on the other hand, if it is false, then it isn't a lie and so must be true!

This paradox, known as the Paradox of the Liar, is usually attributed to Epimenides – although it was actually devised by Eubilides. Epimenides, who was a Cretan, was supposed to have said:

> "All Cretans are liars."

The problem is: Is he telling the truth or not? It seems that if the sentence is true, then it is false. But if it is false, then it is true.

It is easy to miss the point of this paradox. St. Paul, for example, encountered the paradox but seems to miss its force when he writes, "One of themselves, even a prophet of their own, said, 'The Cretans are liars' ...this witness is true." (Titus 1, xii-xiii) Doesn't the supposition that what Epimenides said was true lead to the conclusion that what he said was false and vice versa?

A tempting way out is to suppose that the problem is to do with the notion of self-reference, that Epimenides was referring to himself when he said "All Cretans are liars". After all, one favourite version of the paradox is:

> "This sentence is false."

and a clearer case of self-reference couldn't be given, as the "this" of the sentence refers to the sentence itself.

Such a solution would, however, be premature. On the one hand, not all cases of self-reference are problematic: Epimedides, or anyone else for that matter, may refer to themselves to talk about their height, weight or shoe size; a speaker may say, "Can you hear me at the back?" at the beginning of a talk; a sticker on a rear car bumper may warn, "If you can read this then you're too close." On the other hand, consider the following pair of sentences:

> "The following sentence is true."
> "The preceding sentence is false."

Neither of these sentences refers to itself, and yet the same paradox is generated: if the first sentence is true then it is false – but if it is false then it is true. So the problem can't be about self-reference alone.

Perhaps by now you may be thinking that the problem is that such utterances as Epimenides' and the other versions given above are not true or false but meaningless, that they may, on the surface, appear to make sense but really have no more meaning than the nonsense verse of Lewis Carroll. This solution may also be attractive but consider the following case. You are walking down the street and you find a card on the pavement which says:

"The sentence on the other side of this card is true."

When you turn over the card, the other side reads:

"The sentence on the other side of this card is false."

The problem is that if the first sentence was meaningless then how did you know that you should turn over the card and read the other side...

Also, the appeal to meaninglessness does not avoid a further version of the same paradox, often called the Strengthened Liar, which comes about from considering the following sentence:

"This sentence is either false or meaningless."

Is this sentence true? If it is, then it is either false or meaningless – both options leading to the conclusion that the sentence is not true, for if the sentence is meaningless then it cannot be true. Is it false? If it is, then it is then it is neither false nor meaningless – so it is both true and meaningful.

Diana: The First Perfect Republican?

Rupert Read

Nietzsche: the first perfect nihilist

Friedrich Nietzsche wrote at the opening of *The Will Power* that he considered himself to be "Europe's first perfect nihilist".

For those who have some familiarity with Nietzsche's philosophy, this declaration tends to come as something of a surprise. "Surely," one says to oneself, "Nietzsche was a ferocious *opponent* of nihilism. Surely, for example, he savagely criticised Christianity, and its dead God, precisely on the grounds that it was nihilistic. Surely he wanted instead to argue affirmatively for the vigorous pursuit of life, and for the creation of new values."

Well, yes ... and no. For arguably Nietzsche believed that the creation of new values was only possible once we had thoroughly expunged the old from our systems. And he believed that that was a lot more difficult to achieve than it would be tempting to think. He argued in *The Genealogy of Morals* that science and even atheism are nihilistic, because they still have *faith in truth,* they still believe in a god – Truth. Until we can get beyond such faith, which Nietzsche himself of course shared, and indeed exemplified, Nietzsche holds that we have no chance of creating truly new values, of dancing and affirming in a space beyond good and evil, beyond truth and falsity.

So, what is Nietzsche's solution in *The Genealogy of Morals*? Arguably, it is this: to attack nihilism, but then to reveal that even the attack is still nihilistic because it is exposing the lies involved in religion *etc.,* but *all in the name of a new god,* Truth, and that he, Nietzsche, himself, is in fact the apogee of nihilism. The reader is then encouraged, if s/he can, to start to get beyond both Nietzsche and what Nietzsche criticised, in his or her own way. Nietzsche destroys nihilism, but from the *inside;* like a virus, or a bomb, or an emetic...

He is the perfect nihilist, because he reduces even nihilism (and himself, in the process) to nothing, and thus clears the ground for something new.

Diana: a republican?!

Julie Burchill, shortly after Princess Di's funeral, wrote the following:

> In the soft-focus shampoo commercials being churned out in such indecent haste... [w]e have seen Diana the Good, Diana

the Stylish, Diana the Dutiful.... But we have not yet seen the other great Diana – Diana the Destroyer.

And destroyer she has been, gloriously so, with bells on; the greatest force for republicanism since Oliver Cromwell.

The Guardian, 2 Sept 97 p5

How so? Could such an extravagant claim possibly be justified? "Surely," one says to oneself, "Surely people loved her precisely *because* she was such a lovely *Princess*. And surely *she* didn't want a Republic – she wanted, even at the end, to be the King Mother, the mother of our future King."

Well, yes ... and no. I am not, of course, arguing that she was a republican, an anti-monarchist, *self-consciously*. But I *am* claiming that she *embodied* a devastatingly strong argument for republicanism.

How so?

Well, for sure people loved her because in their/our – in the public's – perception, she was a Princess – and a *human being*.

One might ask this: Why the great grief, if she was indeed recognised to be *a human being,* not semi-divine in the way that royals used to appear to people in days gone by? Why the open, "un-English" grief?

It's surely no coincidence here that she had publicised her *own* grief in recent months and years. That, unlike (for example) Princess Anne, unlike in fact any other royal in living memory – in fact, *ever* – she made it acceptable for a royal, a symbol of the nation, to grieve deeply and openly, to have and express emotion. Further: that she made it acceptable also for a royal to have bulimia, to be in therapy, to be deeply unhappy/depressed, to want a divorce, to want sex and fulfillment; not to mention to be involved with controversial and political causes; the list could go on.

Many, many ordinary people felt close to her, as they never had done to a royal in this country ever – *ever* – because of this. They felt close to her because she was allowing them the forbidden, the *impossible*. That is to say: She was untouchable royalty – *and yet* she was as human as the social worker on the end of the phone, as the teenage Mum next door, as the drug addict hanging out on the street-corner.

She was a Princess, if anyone ever was – *but* she was also someone who did things quite incompatible with everything the principle of monarchy represents. Again, witness her lack of discretion, her lack sometimes of a stiff upper lip, her big-time real-life (soap) drama of heartache and pain, and her (in my view, admirable) involvement in what are frankly political matters (AIDS, Land Mines, *etc.*). She was a royal, and yet not a royal. She was truly royal – but yet she wasn't (like) a royal at all.

People loved her because she was *a contradiction* – "The People's Princess". She had a unique mystique, *because* she and the media circus around her progressively destroyed once and for all the mystique of royalty in this country. She has left the Windsors (ably assisted, it must be said, by Tony Blair and various others) desperately trying to maintain some such mystique, some *raison d'etre* for the monarchy, even while "modernising" and attempting, fairly hopelessly, to "listen to the people". The extraordinary (and in many people's opinions, gobsmackingly hypocritical and despicable) efforts of the Windsors to retrieve Di as "one of them" at the funeral – notably, the draping of the coffin with the Royal Standard, and even the weasel words of Elton John's saccharine song, turning Di into a symbol of England and obliterating her name in the process (while the original version was *all about* the change in Marilyn Monroe's name) – ran into a brick wall at the moments when some diminution of the stiff upper lip was perhaps called for. The Windsors try to retain their difference, their distance, their mystique – *and look worse in the process,* as when they refuse to applaud Earl Spencer's astonishing barn- (or should that be barricade-?) storming speech, when they refuse to cry, when they fail to put their arms around their children. They are caught in the contradiction now, too!

Once more people realise explicitly that Di *was* a contradiction, then they'll realise, as many already have, that she was the Princess who killed the monarchy. The idea of royalty has been unveiled finally as an illusion, as an impossible pose based on nothing. Monarchy in this country has been revealed as having no clothes, has been destroyed by the truth, even if it refuses to admit the fact yet (just as the theistic religions have refused to allow that God is dead). Di was unsustainable, a one-off. I think we all know that the royals we have left to us can't be what she was. The mystique has gone – there's no reason why it should ever come back. The royals are finally, inescapably, irredeemably, human, and ordinary. But there's simply no point in a royal family, no point to all that money and all those pseudo-distinctions, when there's nothing to set that royal family apart from and above the common people. The logic of the humanness of the royals finally being realized – the logic of recognising their kinship with the inhabitants of *Coronation Street* (or at least, of *Dallas*) – points inexorably toward a republic. When "the Queen of Hearts" is loved more than any real queen could be, we have already moved beyond the days of the real monarchy. What is unreal, and dead, ought to lie down.

Diana's child

"But", it will be said, "What about her sons? She can live on through them, with them on the throne. Isn't that, and not a republic, the legacy we ought to want for her, even if sadly she can never now see it realised?"

But, as we heard Earl Spencer movingly speak of protecting those children at Westminster Abbey, and saw them standing there in all their young fragility, and in their inhuman efforts to retain composure, *surely* many of us thought something like this: Do we want anyone, ever again, to have the kind of probably pretty miserable and awful life and death that Diana did, the kind of life which one is so depressed by that one wants out not only of the royal family, but of life itself (her suicide attempts)? Would we really want the Princes – or even the Windsors – to be stuck in the horror-story, in the contradiction, *that she was.* "Even after you died, the Press [that we buy] still hounded your sons..." Does any Diana fan want her sons condemned to be either just like the Windsors who hated her – or else stuck in a horrible and fateful contradiction, between irreconcilable roles, as she was, and as they increasingly are?

Surely not. Once you've seen through the mystique, you don't want to force new children to have to keep on living it, living stuck under its burden. Why should more children have to live that absurd li(f)e; and why should the children of England in general have to continue to grow up living vicariously through and in the shadow of that life of media-images?

Rather than one of her children ascending to the throne, Di's more fitting memorial would be for her to be the first and last people's princess – for there to be no more new princesses, no more princes, and *no more new kings.*

That's why Princess Diana was, as Julie Burchill wrote, "a *glorious* force for republicanism". It's up to her people now to make the republic, and not the flowers and teddy-bears and poems, into her *permanent* memorial.

Thus Diana might very well turn out posthumously to have been this country's first *and last* perfect republican. She could be characterised as a Nietzschean, albeit a slightly unconscious one – for, like him, she embodied a truth that destroyed its nemesis from the inside, by both becoming and exposing it. Nietzsche took nihilism to its logical conclusion, and in him, the anti-nihilistic nihilist, it perished of the truth, of the contradiction, of itself. Princess Di, the impossible human-royal, showed – exposed – the truth of "royalty", and exploded it, like a beautiful firework, that must fade.

Like Nietzsche, and like Christ, and like Socrates, she was a sacrifice. She died, we might even say, for the truth. And her legacy, what she has really given birth to, her true child (of love?), may be a republic – in which her biological children can be ordinary citizens, and not have to live the lie of "royalty".

Burning Questions

Virtually everyone I have met has heard the story of the philosophy exam, where the candidate opened the paper and read, "Is this a question?" The examinee then wrote, "Yes, if this is an answer" and got a First. Does anyone know where this story came from and if it is founded in any truth? And are there any similar stories doing the rounds?

Simon Lee, Edinburgh.

A few years ago our finalist paper had the question, "What is the difference between the earlier and later Wittgenstein?" and a candidate replied "About twenty years".

Name and Address Supplied

A question in an exam was as follows: "Why?" A student answered, "Why not?"

Garry Watters, Belfast

I have heard about an Oxbridge entrance exam that asked people to write an essay to answer the question "What is courage?" The best response given was "this is".

Kirsty Wing

A pal of mine claims to have done very well in first year philosophy on the basis of an exam in which in response to the question, "Why is there something rather than nothing?" he replied, "Because nothing is something".

Arthur O'Neill

The question on my philosophy exam this year read: "If you are a determinist, then your mark for this exam has already been determined and whatever you write will not affect your grade. If you are a fatalist, then why even bother?" I drew a happy face with a dialogue bubble that read I GET AN A. Needless to say, I got an A.

Angela

And I quote...

Nobody is very identical to himself and neither me, but ... neither you. Ha ha! The worst would be that people become identical to themselves. That would be very catastrophical. It's a perpetual game between absence and presence and so on. Then I am not myself and you are not yourself and the world is not itself and, er ... fortunately.

Jean Baudrillard, The Independent on Sunday 11/5/97

God exists, but I don't believe in him. Reality may or may not exist, but I think it is extraordinarily presumptuous to say that things exist just because I do.

Jean Baudrillard, Prospect July 1997

Ever since I developed sense I've been into philosophy. So rather than read books cover to cover, I will read maxims and proverbs which are books in themselves to me. I'll usually have a number on the go which I will dip into. It's fundamental teaching. They have one code to live by – that's more important to me than a novel. Wisdom is what I'm into.

Right now it's Nietzsche. He says: "The weakness of modern personality comes out in the measureless overflow of criticism." This statement justifies my common sense concurring with ideas I've come to accept, in accordance to what I see going on in society. I enjoy reading stuff that's not generally talked about, subliminal things rather than those on the surface. I read philosophy for fun too.

Boxer Chris Eubank, The Guardian 15/4/98

Bertrand Russell refused to use his title because he thought it was elitist.

His son remembers that his childhood home was so unaristocratic that the postman once refused to deliver a telegram to 'the Countess Russell' because he did not believe that the woman on her hands and knees scrubbing the kitchen floor could be who she said she was. 'Yes, and I'm the queen of Persia,' he said.

Rachel Sylvestor, talking to Lord Conrad Russell, son of the great philosopher, Independent on Sunday 13/6/99

Ghosts and Minds

Michael LaBossiere

And this corporeal element, my friend, is heavy and weighty and earthy, and that element of sight by which a soul is depressed and dragged down again into the visible world, because she is afraid of the invisible and of the world below – prowling about tombs and sepulchres, near which, as they tell us, are seen certain ghostly apparitions of souls which have not departed pure, but are cloyed with sight and therefore visible.

Phaedo, by Plato

Everyone has heard of ghosts. Many people believe in them. However, there has not been a great deal of serious philosophical speculation on ghosts. This is not to say that there has been none, since the philosophical issue of ghosts was first discussed in Plato's *Phaedo*. The purpose of this essay is to consider the issue of the existence of ghosts within the context of modern philosophy of mind.

Before it can be decided whether ghosts can exist or not, one must be clear on what it is to be a ghost. For the purpose of this essay, a ghost is a mind which has become disembodied through the death of its original body, yet still has the capacity to interact with the physical world in some manner. This interaction might be that the ghost can be sensed by others or that the ghost can actually manipulate its physical environment or perhaps some other capacity for interaction.

It should be noted that it has not been assumed that a ghost must be an immaterial entity. This is because assuming that ghosts must be immaterial would beg the question at hand. Thus, the possibility that ghosts could be material entities (of a special sort) must be kept open.

There are a variety of philosophic theories which attempt to explain the mind. Some of the more popular and famous ones include the identity theory, substance dualism, property dualism and functionalism. The implications of these theories will be considered in turn.

Identity theory is a materialist theory of mind, which is to say that it is a view that takes the mind to be composed of matter. More specifically, those who accept the identity theory assert that each mental state is identical to a state of the central nervous system. Thus, the mind is equivalent to the central nervous system and its states. Given the nature of identity theory, it is clear that if it is correct, then there are no ghosts. This is because the death of the central nervous system would be the death and end of the mind, because they are identical.

Substance dualism is the view that reality contains at least two fundamental types of entities: material entities and immaterial entities. On this view, which was most famously presented by Descartes, the mind is an immaterial substance which enjoys a special sort of causal relation with its body. This rather mysterious relation enables the mind to control and receive information from the body and allows the body to affect the mind in some respects. Not surprisingly, on this view ghosts are a real possibility. Since the mind is taken to be a separate substance, the death of the body need not result in the death of the mind. Since the mind is a distinct substance and substances are entities that are capable of independent existence, the mind could, in theory, continue to exist. Further, since the mind is assumed to be able to interact with its original body, it is also possible that the mind could continue to interact with the physical world even in its bodiless state. Presumably, the lack of a physical body could limit what the mind was capable of, which might explain why ghosts are often taken to be limited in their capabilities. For example, it is typically believed that ghosts are often limited to making faint noises, moving small objects, or creating annoying thumping and banging noises.

A second type of dualism is sometimes refererred to as property dualism. On this view, the mind and body are not distinct substances. Instead, the mind is composed (at least in part) of mental properties that are not identical with physical properties. For example, the property of *being a painful feeling* could not be reduced to a particular physical property of the brain, such as the states of certain neurons. Thus, the mind and body are distinct, but are not different substances.

Property dualism has a long history and, not surprisingly, there are many varieties of this view, two of which will be considered here. One of these versions is consistent with the existence of ghosts and the other is not.

Property dualism splits, roughly, into two main camps, epiphenomenalism and interactionism.

Epiphenomenalism is the view that there is a one-way relation between the mental and physical properties. On this view, the non-physical mental properties are caused by, but do not in turn cause, the physical properties of the body. On this view, the mind is causally inert and is, crudely speaking, a by-product of the physical processes of the body. Because the mental properties are causally dependent on the physical properties, the death of the body will result in an end to the mental properties. Hence, if epiphenomenalism is correct, then there are no ghosts.

Interactionism is, in this context, the view that the mental properties of the mind and physical properties of the body interact. On this view mental properties can bring about changes in the physical properties of the body and vice versa. Unlike epiphenomenalism, interactionism does not require that the mental properties be entirely causally dependent on the physical properties of the original body. Because of this, the mental properties that compose the mind could, in theory, survive the death of the original body. These mental properties might be capable of existing as a bundle of properties. In this case, a ghost would be a bundle of mental properties that forms a mind without any physical body. The mental properties might require some substance or body to support them. In this case, a ghost would be a mind that consists of mental properties that are supported by something other than its original body. For example, the mental properties might inhere in an object or place. This might explain the fact that ghosts are typically said to haunt particular places. If their minds inhere in these places, this would explain why ghosts rarely, if ever, travel about the world. As another possibility, the mental properties might take control of a new body. This might explain cases that purportedly involve possession. In any case, since the mental properties are supposed to be capable of interaction with physical properties, it would be possible for the mind to continue to interact with the physical world, despite the death of its original body.

One last view to be considered is functionalism. There are many varieties of functionalism, but they all share a common basis. This basis is that mental states are defined in functional terms. Roughly put, a functional definition of a mental state defines that mental state in terms of its role or function in a mental system of inputs and outputs. To be a bit more specific, a mental state, such as being in pain, is defined in terms of the causal relations that it holds to external influences on the body, other mental states, and the behaviour of the body.

Functionalism is typically regarded as a materialist view of the mind. This is because the systems in which the mental states take place are taken to be physical systems. While the identity theory and functionalism are both materialist theories of mind, they differ in one key respect. According to the identity theorists, a specific mental state, such as being in pain, is identical to a specific physical state, such as the state of neurons in a particular part of the brain. So, for two mental states to be the same, the physical states must be identical. Thus, if mental states are particular states of neurons in a certain part of the human nervous system then anything that does not have that sort of nervous system cannot have a mind. According to the functionalist, a specific mental state, such as being in pain, is not defined in terms of a particular physical state. Instead, while the functionalist believes that every mental state is a physical state of some kind, for two mental states to be the same they need only be functionally identical, not physically identical. Thus, if mental states are defined functionally, then anything that can exhibit these functions, can have a mind.

As odd as it might sound, if functionalism is the correct theory of mind, then it is still possible for ghosts to exist. This is the case even if it is assumed that functionalism must be a materialist theory of mind. As noted above, functionalism is committed to the view that any system that performs the proper functions is a mind, regardless of how that system is constituted. Given this, it seems possible that a mind could suffer the loss of its original physical system, yet still retain the same or adequately similar functions after this loss. Since the mind is, on the functionalist account, a physical system, there would be no special problem with it interacting with the physical world, even after it has a new physical system. The new physical system might be a structure, place or a new body. For example, a person might die in a house and, consistent with many ghost stories, the mind of the person might survive in the house. In functionalist terms, the mind that was once a set of functions instantiated in a human body would now be a set of functions instantiated in a house or parts of a house. As long as the functions are preserved, the mind would continue to exist as a ghost. Since ghosts are typically said to be confined to particular places, even particular rooms, the functionalist account of ghosts has a certain plausibility.

While the issue of the actual existence or non-existence of ghosts has not been settled, this essay has addressed the issue of the existence of ghosts within the context of modern philosophy of mind. If dualism, property dualism or functionalism is correct, then ghosts can exist. However, if identity theory is correct, then there can be no ghosts.

Paradoxes
2: Russell's Paradox
Francis Moorcroft

The British Library sends out instructions that every library in the country has to make a catalogue of all its books. Each librarian makes their catalogue and are then faced with a choice: the catalogue is, after all, a book in their library; should the title of the catalogue be included in the catalogue itself or not? Some librarians decide to include it, others not to.

In the course of time the catalogues are sent to the British Library and the chief librarian there has the job of making a catalogue of these catalogues. But they find that they have two different sorts of catalogues to deal with: those that mention themselves inside the catalogue and those that don't. That is, they have catalogues that contain their own titles and catalogues that don't. So the chief librarian decides to make two different catalogues corresponding to these two different kinds. With the catalogue of all those catalogues that include themselves the librarian has the choice to include the title of the catalogue in itself or not. No problem there. But with the catalogue of catalogues that *don't* include themselves the librarian is faced with a dilemma: should they include the title of the catalogue in the catalogue or not? if they *do* then it is not a catalogue that does not contain its own title and so it shouldn't be included; if they don't put it in then it is a catalogue that doesn't contains its own title and so should be included. Either way, it should contain itself if it doesn't and shouldn't contain itself if it does!

This paradox is a version of Russell's Paradox. It came about from Bertrand Russell thinking about the notion of a set, or class, or collection of things, and whether a set can be a member of itself or not. For example, think about the totality of cats in the world: this is the set of cats. Is this set a member of itself or not. Clearly not – it's a set, an abstract object, not a cat. But now think about all of the things in the world that are *not* cats - dogs, chairs, books, violin sonatas, ... and sets. This set is a member of itself. Now it is far more usual for a set to *not* be a member of itself than for it to be a member of itself. Let's call sets that don't belong to themselves *normal*. Now Russell's problem is: is the set of all normal sets a member of itself or not? If it is then it isn't. But if it isn't then it is...

Russell's own solution to the problem is his Theory of Types. This can be explained as follows. Imagine that five people get together to form a five-a-side football team. This team then joins a local league, and the league in turn is part of a regional association. Clearly, an individual can only be member of a team and cannot be a member of a league or an association: it is the wrong *type* of thing, as only teams can be members of leagues and leagues members of associations. Similarly, Russell thought that individuals, type C, were members of sets or classes of type 1. These sets could only be members of sets of type 2, and sets of type 2 could only be members of the higher type 3, and so on. Specifically, a set could not belong to another set of the same type, as it has to belong to a set of the next highest type, and so a set can never be a member of itself.

While the Theory of Types does work as a solution to the Paradox many logicians feel that it has an *ad hoc* air about it, and isn't as intuitively obvious as is required for the foundations of mathematics: after all, Russell's solution may seem plausible for football teams but mathematics does consider sets that are formed from individuals, sets of individuals, sets of sets of individuals and so on, and counting out such sets seems to be a high price to pay for avoiding the Paradox.

Readers may wonder whether Russell's Paradox is a problem only in the foundations of mathematics or if it actually occurs in real life. I recently saw a policy concerning disability which contained a number of clauses naming specific disabilities which were included under the policy. The last clause, however, contained the statement "Other disabilities not on this is list". Now consider a specific disability not named in the list: if it was not on this list then this clause includes it in the list so it *is* on the list; if it is on the list then the clause says it is *not* on the list. Without care, paradoxes can occur where we least expect them.

THE PROBLEM WITH KNOWLEDGE..

Burning Questions

Is there any correlation between philosophy and depression?

Marianne Di Napoli, Ramsgate.

Yes, but there's no point in investigating it. It won't make things any better.

Robin Harwood

Julia Kristeva claims that periods of depression are phases we have to go through to reach higher states of consciousness. Depression is a creative process, and she means that this explains (to a certain degree) why artists so often are depressive and also suicidal.

Submitted by email

A study done a few years ago highlighted that those studying philosophy as a university degree had the highest rate of suicide amongst the students. Is there a connection then between negative thought processes which could lead to individuals suffering from depression or even committing suicide and the study of philosophy? My personal belief is that those who undertake the heavy task of studying philosophy possibly have a very different mental inquisitiveness and also may have a greater need to find subjective truths or meaning. Thus the result is a body of people studying a subject, in which they hope to find answers or possibly just begin with asking questions. In R Harpers book *The Existential Experience* he explores why some people are more prone to exploring their interior life than others and concluded that, "lacking a foundation of self knowledge, they should not be expected to feel the urgency of existential questions."

Maybe the process of depression and the cave it leaves in an individual paves the way for philosophical speculation, rather than philosophy being the prime cause of that depression.

D. Sutherland

My common-sense answer would be that people who begin to study philosophy in the first place are generally of above average perceptual and mental sensitivity, generally introverted, and hence are more likely to suffer depression than people who are less sensitive.

Patrick S

And I quote...

The most quoted philosopher in our regular 'Mediawtch' column – Roger Scruton

My wife Sophie and I have decided to offer Sam a genuinely deprived childhood. [...] Childhood is not an end in itself but a means to growing up. Sam is to emerge from his ordeal with the kind of character that arouses sympathy, and with the virtues that engender respect.

The Guardian 28/4/99

As soon as people make judgements in the modern world they're dismissed as judgemental. I don't mind being called judgemental but I do make distinctions between those things that are worth attending to and those things that are not.

In Our Time, BBC Radio Four 21/1/99

Chattering through the speeches of their peers, with their feet on the benches and sneers on their faces, they typify the football hooligans and pop fans who voted for their party and who could not tell a debate from a debenture.

on Labour Members of Parliament

Most people who ride horses don't actually ride horses – a horse doesn't exist as an individual. It's one cell in a potential organism and that organism has to be completed, as it is when the herd is present, racing across country, itself animated by its own primeval forces. And there, in that environment, you recognise that you too are an animal.

Start the Week, BBC Radio 4 12/10/98

Life for a child is easy if he can avoid adults together and at a family meal he can't. That's not a bad thing.

The Observer 5/9/99

Delia Smith is, actually, my *bête noire*. I consider her a most pernicious influence. She gives the impression cooking is all about measuring, whereas it isn't. It's about smell, texture, improvisation.

The Independent 14/12/98

Cloning and Immortality

Robin Harwood

Shortly after the announcement that British scientists had successfully cloned a sheep, *The Guardian* ran an article about a man who thought that cloning could provide a route to immortality The article did not include a detailed account of how this was to be achieved, but the essential idea is that since in cloning the genetic blueprint for a particular individual is used to make another individual with the same genetic makeup, the new individual will be an exact copy of the original, and an exact copy is as good as the original.

Thus, the suggestion is that we can bring back the dead by cloning them. All we need is a few cells removed from the body just before death, and we can use these to produce a person with the same genetic makeup, so, in a way, recreating the dead person. In this way, if I can have myself cloned, I can make sure that after my death there will be someone with the same genetic makeup as myself, who will be an exact copy of me. Having this exact copy made is the same as being resurrected, which, if the process is continued, will give me immortality.

An alternative way of achieving immortality through cloning is the rather grisly one of using a clone as a source of spare parts. Well before my eyes start to fade, and my heart starts to falter, I have a clone of myself produced. When this clone is, say, seventeen, I have his eyes and heart transplanted into me. This transplant will probably be successful, since there is less likelihood of the transplanted parts being rejected, because they are genetically identical to my own heart and eyes. Similarly if I keep having clones produced, there will spares for any bit of me that wears out. Thus, I will be able to live for ever. (We may be able to get the spare parts by a different sort of cloning, in which bits of my tissue are cultivated into spare organs in tanks. This might be preferable to chopping up a seventeen-year-old boy for parts.)

The question is, do either of these suggestions actually provide the sort of immortality we usually want? To answer this question, we must decide what we want from immortality. Now it is possible that different people want different things, so I will have to answer for myself, but I suspect that in this, at least, I am not much different from most people. I do not just want my body to last (in good condition) forever, or my name to be honoured for all time. The most important part of wanting to live forever is, for me at least, wanting to experience the future of that immortal life in the same direct way that I experience the present.

The way I have my experiences now is as part of the present stream of consciousness. To have future experiences in the same way, those future experiences must be part of the same stream. That is, the present stream must continue and eventually include those experiences, so that the experiences I am having now will overlap with further experiences in a chain of overlapping experiences that ultimately includes the future experiences. In short, what I want is the infinite continuation of my stream of consciousness, the stream of consciousness of which my present experience is part. This continuity is a necessary condition for my survival. Without it, I do not survive.

An obvious objection here is to say that my stream of consciousness is interrupted every time I go to sleep, and yet I believe that I have survived that interruption. If the continuity of my stream of consciousness really is a necessary condition of my survival, I would have to admit that I will not survive tonight's sleep. In reply, I will first point out that I believe (as did Descartes) that in fact the stream of consciousness continues during sleep, even if we do not always remember it. This view is supported by the results of psychological experiments on sleep, including studies in which people woken from various stages of sleep were able to report what they had been thinking while asleep, but I will not discuss it in detail here. Second, even if the stream of consciousness does not continue during sleep, there certainly seems to be some sort of strong continuity between the me who went to sleep and the me who wakes up to the extent that my present stream of consciousness seems to be a continuation of the stream of consciousness I had yesterday. Thus, I can amend my claim to say that what I want is the infinite continuation of my stream of consciousness, or, if there are any interruptions in my stream of consciousness, there must be at least the same sort of continuity as that between going to sleep and waking up, whatever that continuity might consist in. If I can arrange that infinite continuation of my stream of consciousness, I will have the most important part of immortality. I will survive forever.

Can I get this by having a clone of myself made? If my stream of consciousness ceases when I die, and a stream of consciousness starts when the clone is produced, will my stream of consciousness be continuous with his? I cannot see how it could be. The clone's stream of consciousness will develop with the clone, but have no connection with mine. Thus, the stream of consciousness of the clone is not the continuation of my stream of consciousness. Now since I have established that worthwhile immortality requires the continuation of my stream of consciousness, simply creating a clone of me does not provide immortality. I have to find some way of transferring my stream of consciousness to the clone, and my stream of consciousness must either remain uninterrupted during the transfer or at least have the same sort of continuity as that between going to sleep and waking up.

It has been suggested that the continuity can be created by in some way recording all my memories, ideas, personality traits, and thoughts and then putting all the information into the clone's brain. This sort of recording was done with Lister in the television show *Red Dwarf*, and at first blush it seems convincing enough. After all, we are used to our memories, ideas, etc., always accompanying our stream of consciousness, and so we usually think that they will stay together. Where one goes, there the rest will go. But it is not necessarily so. Here is an imaginary case to try to demonstrate this. (This example is adapted from Unger, 1986, and Knox, 1969.)

(Part 1) I collapse onto the floor. Then I find that I seem to be floating up out of my body and hovering near the ceiling, looking down on my body, as in the standard accounts of out-of-body experience. The body on the floor begins to move. It gets up and acts, talks, and shows that consciousness is again associated with the body. There are two conscious beings. One is me, floating near the ceiling, and the other is the being with the body that used to be mine.

(Part 2) While floating away from the body I suddenly lose my personal memory (memory of my past life, as distinct from memory of the English language) and my personality changes. The being in what used to be my body appears to have memories qualitatively similar to the memories I had, and a personality qualitatively similar to the personality I had.

In part 1 I consider my survival to be independent of my body. I survive as the floating being, not the one that inhabits the body I thought of as mine, because the stream of consciousness of the floating being is continuous with my stream of consciousness before I collapsed.

In part 2 the being in my body has physical continuity with the person I was, and has greater psychological continuity with the exception of the continuity of conscious experience. All my friends will think that I simply fainted. The conscious being acts like I used to and can remember the things I used to. Possibly even he thinks that he is a continuation of me. Yet in this case also I consider that I survive as the floating being, not the embodied one, because of the continuity of the stream of consciousness. If, before the collapse, I knew it was going to happen, and I also knew that after the collapse, the floating being would suffer the tortures of Hell, I would feel genuine fear, because I would expect to suffer the tortures of Hell in exactly the same direct way I am suffering the tortures of writing a philosophy paper now.

In other words, it seems that my memories, etc., can go one way, and my stream of consciousness can go another. If this is so, then when I am linked up to the device which transfers my memories, etc. to the clone, there is no guarantee that it will also transfer my stream of consciousness.

Also, there is an interruption between the end of my stream of consciousness and the start of the clone's stream of consciousness, but there is no guarantee that the interruption will be bridged by the sort of continuity we have during sleep. We do not know what provides that continuity, so we cannot assume that the recording process would provide it. (In ordinary sleep my body and brain do not cease to exist and do not cease to function. It is quite reasonable to suggest that their continuity is the foundation for the continuity I feel between the me who went to sleep and the me who wakes up. If I die, my body and brain cease to function. Alternatively, if I am right and the stream of consciousness of a living person never ceases, even during sleep, then again the recording process will not provide the necessary continuity.)

Just producing a clone of me will not give me immortality. From this it follows, that if the clone does not provide a way for me to be recreated after my death, then of course it does not provide a way of recreating other dead people either. A clone of Mozart will have the same genetic makeup as Mozart, but it will not be Mozart.

However, there does seem to be a way I can use cloning to live forever, and that is by a special use of the cloned spare parts. There is no theoretical problem about replacing most parts, but when we come to the brain it is a different story. As my old brain wears out, I need to replace it with the new brain. The trouble is that, for the reasons outlined above, I have to transfer my stream of consciousness to the new brain, and it is not clear how I can do that. Still, there does seem to be a way around the problem. If I cannot transfer my stream of consciousness to the new brain, I can get the same result by transferring the new brain to my stream of consciousness. I need to find a way of taking out tiny bits of my old brain, and replacing them with tiny bits from the new brain, while I am conscious. Each tiny piece would have to be so small that its removal would not affect the continuity of my stream of consciousness. If we can do this, eventually all the old brain would be replaced by the new brain, without any interruption to my stream of consciousness.

Perhaps when the bits of my brain are being replaced, I will find that my personality changes, and perhaps some or all of my memories or skills are lost. This would be regrettable, but it is the sort of thing that happens anyway. As I get older at least some aspects of my personality change (usually for the worse) and some of my memories disappear. (Especially, but not solely, memories of what my wife told me to do this morning.) If the piecemeal brain replacement were similar, but I could still form new memories, regain skills or gain new ones, and form a personality no more inadequate than the one I have now, I would not object too strongly. Indeed, there are some memories I would be happier without.

This imaginary technique seems to be the most probable way that we can gain immortality from any sort of cloning, but it is a long way from anything that is possible at the moment. Indeed, even when the technique of transplanting bits of brain is perfected, it is still not clear that it will be possible. We may find, for example, that there is some bit of the brain that cannot be disconnected without interrupting the stream of consciousness. We have a long way to go from Dolly to immortality.

Paradoxes
3: The hangman
Francis Moorcroft

In a harsh totalitarian country an innocent person is arrested on Sunday evening and summarily condemned to execution, which they are told will take place on one of the following five mornings. To make matters worse, they are told that they will not know the day before which morning it will be. After several hours torment the prisoner fails into a peaceful sleep as they realise that such a threat cannot be carried out. They reasoned thus:

The execution cannot take place on Friday morning; for if they are still alive on Thursday night then the execution must take place on Friday. But they were told that they would not know the day before which day it would be. So it cannot be Friday, and so Friday can be counted out as a possibility. But by the same reasoning it cannot be Thursday either. For if they are still alive on Wednesday night then the execution must take place on Thursday. But they were told that they would not know the day before which day it would be. So it cannot be Thursday, and so Thursday can be counted out as a possibility. But by the same reasoning it cannot be Wednesday either... The same reasoning covers Wednesday, Tuesday and Monday and so the prisoner can have a sound night's sleep.

The prisoner is, however, greatly surprised to find themselves facing the executioner on Wednesday (or indeed any other) morning. What went wrong with the prisoner's reasoning?

This paradox, known as the Hangman, is an instance of the Paradox of Prediction. Another instance is the Surprise Exam: a teacher tells the class that there will be an exam sometime during the term but the students will not know the day before when it will be; it can't be last day of term – if the second to last day has been finished with no exam then it must be this day and so no surprise – nor can it be the second to last day for the same reason, and so on through the other days of term. Yet we know that surprise examinations do occur.

Both the Hangman and the Surprise Exam have a common form, that is:

> You will be hung one morning this week (there will be a surprise exam during term) but you cannot predict on the basis of this statement what day that will be.

This statement is clearly self-referential and we know from previous experience (see The Paradox of the Liar and Russell's Paradox) that such statements are problematic. But is self-reference all that is causing the problems here?

As well as self-reference, the paradox also involves prediction and prediction involves knowledge and knowledge involves truth. Consider the following

> No-one knows this proposition.

Is this true or false? If it is false then someone does know the proposition. But knowing something implies what is known is true, and so the proposition is true. Hence we have shown that the proposition is true and therefore we now know it to be true. So if we know it to be true then someone knows it to be true, you and I now know it to be true, for example, and so it is false!

So is the problem more to do with knowledge, specifically the prisoner's claim to knowledge? Suppose that the prisoner is told on Sunday evening that you will be hung tomorrow at dawn but you will not know that beforehand. Can such a sentence be carried out? The prisoner may claim that such a sentence is self-contradictory but is this simply the prisoner making a mistaken claim to knowledge – which fact would be shown by the sentence being carried out. To be sure, the prisoner has a belief that the sentence cannot be carried out but a belief – and certainly as in this case a false belief – is a long way from knowledge. The sentence only claims that the prisoner will remain in ignorance up until the time of the actual hanging: but there remains the possibility that the sentence is a cruel joke intended to further torment the prisoner.

The prisoner is only allowed to argue with regard to the above sentence

> If it is true then I will know I will be hung in advance.

And the prisoner does not know whether the judge who issued the sentence spoke truly or not. Only when the hanging occurs does it becomes clear that rather than a mere possibility, it is an actual fact.

This response argues that the prisoner is claiming to know more than they are entitled to claim, and here lies the fallacy in the prisoner's reasoning. The claim must be wrong because surprise hangings (or examinations) do occur.

One point about this reply to the Paradox of Prediction: It supposes that there are statements that are true or false – but that we cannot know which. Consider a prediction that is made, not about tomorrow or next week or the end of term but about some time in the far future when we will not be here to see the outcome: does it make sense to say that the prediction is true or false if we cannot tell which?

Burning questions

Is there any truth in the words of Monty Python's philosophers' drinking song?

Daisy Sinclair

There is, so far as I know, no truth to the sentiment expressed in the Philosopher's Drinking Song, to wit that the pantheon of philosophy, Socrates to Wittgenstein, was populated by inebriates. Plato and Socrates probably had their moments, and I can't vouch for Descartes or Mill, but Kant was famously boring and Wittgenstein was anything but a beery swine, though one can't help but think that a glass or two of wine might not have been a bad idea for him on occasion.

Keep in mind it is the *Australian* Philosopher's Drinking Song; I think what we have here is a post-modern reconstruction of the philosophical canon with an eye toward laying down a moral foundation from which could be defended a view of philosophy which involves fitting one's entire mouth around a can of Fosters before 10:00 AM.

Gary Hardcastle

No, there is no truth in the words of the Monty Python drinking song, because truth is a property of sentences, not of words. (And yes, I do mean sentences, not propositions. I'll explain why to anyone who buys me a beer.)

Roderick T. Lon

According to the song, 'Immanuel Kant was a real *pissant* who was very rarely stable'. *Au contraire* – Kant was so stable that the residents of Konigsberg allegedly set their watches by him. The only thing that ever upset Kant's routine was not a litre of full proof whiskey, but reading Rousseau's *Emile*. Hardly a rock and roll lifestyle. This is further substantiated by Scruton's claim that Kant ordered his footman to wake him up at five every morning and 'tolerate no malingering'. That is not the action of a man with frequent hangovers.

Socrates must have been quite accomplished in the bar, for the following reasons: Having been condemned by an Athenian jury to die by drinking hemlock, Plato describes Socrates as drinking it and then proceeding to hold some highly rational discussions with his mates. This is odd, from the point of view that drinking hemlock normally induces spasms, cramp, nausea, and a general inability to do anything before killing you horribly. So if Socrates dealt with it so well, he must have been used to necking some pretty strong stuff.

Lambert Williams, London

Bizarre news

It sounds like an idea for a Python sketch – French philosopher decides to make a film. But rather than being a meditation on deep philosophical issues, it seems that the director is more interested in sex scenes where the principal actress is his wife.

The film in question is *Le Jour et la Nuit*, directed by Bernard-Henri Levy. Starring top-notch French talents like Oscar winner Alain Delon, Lauren Bacall and, er, Arielle Dombassie (Levy's wife), the film was savaged by critics and booed by audiences at the Berlin Film Festival.

"The camera," said Levy, "has allowed me to express, better than I have done before, my love for women and their bodies." The critics did not agree. *Libération* compared the film to "adolescent fantasies when you pinned up 'playmate of the month' on your bedroom wall," while *Le Parisien* said Levy "is a writer and should stick to that."

Delon stuck up for the film, saying "I think it was one of the best films I was able to play in my entire career." M. Bacall, however, when asked if it was her least favourite film simply replied, "That is an amusing question."

Levy is a famous figure in France, where philosophers are more highly regarded than they are in Britain. He often appears on television chat shows, and with his sleek dark mane and unbuttoned shirt, is about as rock 'n roll as a philosopher could get.

This contrasts with his reputation in Britain, where he doesn't even merit an entry in the authoritative *Oxford Companion to Philosophy*. He represents the kind of all-round French intellectual which perhaps only Anthony Burgess came close to emulating in Britain, and whom analytic philosophers dismiss as "unphilosophical".

Levy himself has been phlegmatic about the film's poor reviews. "I think they tell us more about the state of mind of the people who write them than about the quality of the film," he said.

From The news pages of TPM1

Thinking with your feet
Simon Walter

In the introduction to his particularly funny commentary, *Philosophy Football* (Penguin), which describes "what might have happened to the world's greatest thinkers if their brains had been in their boots instead of their heads", Mark Perryman relates how the idea first came to him to couple football with philosophy. He tells of how, inspired by the desire to become the "sporting outfitters of intellectual distinction", he contrived a goalkeeper's shirt emblazoned with a quotation. "All that I know most surely about morality and obligations, I owe to football." This sagacity, of course, is ascribed to Albert Camus, the most famous practitioner of the complementary arts of thinking and keeping a clean sheet. The success of this idea has led to a proliferation of shirts and a thriving trade that retails the aphorisms of such disparate thinkers as Antonio Gramsci, Umberto Eco, Sun Tzu and Simone de Beauvoir.

The book that accompanies the series, *Philosophy Football* is a q*uasi una fantasia*, where "Eleven great thinkers play it deep". It is indeed an imaginative interpretation of the philosophical positions of the aforementioned in terms of qualities recognisable to the followers, of what Pele called, the "beautiful game". My favourite example comes from the chapter on Wittgenstein. "Opponents found his game difficult to read. In fact, everyone found him difficult to read."

However, it is not the case that the two disparate activities of philosophy and football have never been brought together before for humorous effect. An early *Monty Python* sketch memorably staged a match between Germany and Greece that ended prematurely when Nietzsche, arguing with the referee, called into question the very purpose of the contest. Nevertheless, while the affinity between philosophy and football is easily established, it occurred to me, as I read Perrymann's book, that football was being used as a very malleable illustration of more general philosophical positions. This is all very agreeable and engaging but it neglects the inherent characteristics of the sport that make it what it is. In other words, I began to wonder whether there was a discrete philosophy of football, a set of concepts and questions intrinsic to the understanding and contemplation of the game, a specific branch of philosophical thinking comparable to the discipline of Aesthetics or Ethics.

Pondering this conjecture and taking a tip from Pele rather than Camus, it seemed to me that art not morality may be the most appropriate place to begin. The thought suggested itself that, football, like art, is a kind of performance appreciated through the categories *of form* and *content,* which are discriminated for the purposes of analysis but in practice are indistinguishable. From the perspective of form, football clubs confront each other in a manner comparable to that moment in Hegel's *Philosophy Of The Right* when the state evolves into the idea of a "nation". "Nationhood" is understood in terms of individual qualities, a subject in its own right, a spiritual identity derived from geography and the general will of the people. Thus Perryman's club, Tottenham Hotspur, represents itself to itself and to the football public at large through certain quintessential attributes. In the case of Spurs this is the romance of the *Glory Game,* a cavalier style of play associated with the club's most successful season. This differentiates it from its competitors, the more pragmatic or defensively orientated sides, such as the traditionally "boring" Arsenal.

The *spirit* of the club is a synthesis of locality and history that transcends the particularity of the current crop of players and those responsible for the day to day running of the corporation. The most important role is that of the manager. Indeed, although the validity of the Cartesian subject has been successively brought into question by thinkers from the continental tradition, football, phenomenologically, seems to refute this scepticism. Duality is alive and well in the manner that football is reflected upon by those who reflect upon it. The *mind* of the manager finds expression through the actions of the *body* of players on the field. This model of volition, essentially Aristotelian, is confirmed by the assignment of praise or blame for the success or failure of the team. There is never any question about who deserves the credit for the performance of the players. The stoic acceptance of the inevitability of being sacked gives the manager the appearance of a tragic protagonist, the individual who sacrifices themselves for a higher ideal, the catalyst and dynamo of the German Idealist conception of History. Thus the narrative that the club tells of its illustrious past is marked in terms of epochs, the successive tenures of managers, for instance the eras of Shankly, Paisley and Dalglish at Liverpool.

This concept of agency finds its apotheosis the *Science* of football, the harnessing of technology and psychology with tactics, as practised by the Dynamo Kiev coach Valerie Lobonovski. His accomplice is Professor Anatoly Zelentsov. Together they were the brains behind the formidable Soviet national team of the late eighties, the appropriately nicknamed, *Red Machine*. It is here that the *form* and *content* of the philosophy of football coalesce. Its substance, the concrete embodiment of the *Idea,* the particular football match, appears to be a spontaneous spectacle, but like art, is in fact the product of deliberation.

Although the intentional relationship between artist and art object is a problem for aesthetics, not so for football. Tactics and realisation are more intimately bound than score and performance in music. The historic vindication of this idea is the knighthood bestowed on Alf

Ramsey and the current enthusiasms for the sport amongst the public at large.

It is no coincidence that the game's popularity has spread to all social classes since the introduction of continental players and coaches. Becoming cosmopolitan has enabled football to relinquish its working class roots and thus broaden its appeal. Traditionally system builders with exotic names, like their philosophical counterparts, European minds such as Ruud Guilit and Arsene Wenger, have maintained a conceptual integrity, a consistency between theory and practice, that approaches the conventional definition of a philosophy. In the former's case a derivative of the Left Hegelianism of Dutch *total football,* named by Guilit himself – *Sexy Football.*

Could football's allure simply be the same as that of philosophy in that it seeks to overcome the contradictions of reality? This is why Mark Perryman's book works so well and why, unfortunately, Eric Cantona's analogies were not as pretentious as they first appear. Football is best understood as a contemporary equivalent of Kant's *aesthetic idea. Form* confers a recognisable purpose upon the object of contemplation, a teleology that engages the understanding, which is ultimately undermined, in genuine works of art, by a purposeless *content* inspiring the imagination. So it is with football, only in a more exaggerated manner. The comic Nietzsche in the *Monty Python* sketch was mistaken to question the point of the game. For like art, the very fact that it takes place confirms a metaphysical yearning, a *spiritual* desire on the part of a people for a coherent destiny, a destiny whose point is that it is pointless. If that seems a little far-fetched, watch the World Cup next summer.

33

And I quote...

I find myself in a position of contradiction, not unknown in the history of philosophy. I feel on the one hand that five million frogs, as some say, can't all be wrong – there must be something in French philosophy. I'm inclined to think that it's such a different sort of think to British or American philosophy that it has to be looked at differently. One thinks of French philosophy that it aspires to the condition of literature or the condition of art, and that English and American philosophy aspires to the condition of science. French philosophy, one thinks of as picking up an idea and running with it, possibly into a nearby brick wall or over a local cliff, or something like that. That is one difference – we're much more restrained.

Ted Honderich, Radio Four's Today programme 5/12/98

Jean-François Lyotard agreed to be on a television programme with Bricmont and me and we had a kind of debate. Unfortunately it wasn't a very serious programme. Also, unfortunately the fifteen minute debate consisted of a ten-minute monologue by Lyotard in very flowery French, in which, if I understood him correctly, he said that physicists don't understand that words are used in a different way in poetry and novels than they are in physics books. When we finally got to the floor, we said, "Well, we know that, but to our knowledge the books of Lacan and Delouze are not sold in the poetry section of bookstores, they are sold in psychology and philosophy, so they should be judge by the standards of psychology and philosophy – those are cognitive discourses, they are purporting to say something about something, let's judge them that way. If you want to re-classify them as poetry, then we can judge them on whether they're good poetry or not." My personal feeling would be most of these people don't write good poetry either.

Physicist Alan Sokal, Interviewed in TPM4

I went to the Beauborg to have dinner with him [Derrida]. I think his students had played him the 'Derrida' single when it first came out and he'd been intrigued by it ever since. He claimed to have kept up with any press about me.

Pop musician Green Gartside, aka Scritti Politti, to John O'Reilly,
The Independent 16/7/99

I did not write a book about Albert Camus' love life. Even a telephone directory wouldn't have been long enough for that!

Camus' biographer Oliver Todd, Independent on Sunday 5/10/97

Popper and the Poker
News, TPM3

An extraordinary row has broken out as to whether or not one of the giants of western philosophy lost his temper in a now mythical meeting of the Cambridge Moral Science Club in October 1946. Professor John Watkins of the London School of Economics resuscitated the row in a recent British Academy lecture on Karl Popper. Professor Watkins claims that the incident occurred after Wittgenstein and Popper had been arguing as to whether there are any genuine philosophical problems, as opposed to mere puzzles. "Popper gave the question of the validity of moral rules. Wittgenstein, who had hold of the poker and was waving it about a good deal, demanded an example of a moral rule, to which Popper replied: 'Not to threaten visiting lecturers with pokers.' There was laughter and Wittgenstein stormed out."

Within the pages of the *Times Literary Supplement*, denials and counter-assertions have been flying. Peter Geach, present at the meeting, claims "this story is false from beginning to end", while John Vienlott, also present, claims the story is essentially true, but has been embellished somewhat.

What the row really reveals is that the differences between philosophers, in this case Popper and Wittgenstein , are often far more than of mere opinion, and that these antipathies are often carried on by their followers.

The Philosophers' Magazine asked Professor Watkins why the story refuses to lie down and still arouses so much passion. His reply sheds interesting light on the controversy:

"If the story arouses strong passions that's presumably because it has the makings of a myth, David-and-Goliath style. Here's the set-up. Wittgenstein (although he has published virtually nothing since the *Tractatus*), dominates Cambridge, and indeed English, philosophy, and the Moral Science Club is very much his territory. Enter Karl Popper, a younger man who has arrived in England only recently. (His *The Open Society* has been published for nearly a year but it's not clear that many of those present will have read it.) In his sling he carries refutations of the Wittgensteinian thesis that there are no genuine philosophical problems. Also conspicuously present is Bertrand Russell, reinstalled in Trinity after his wartime exile in America. He had once dominated Cambridge philosophy but has been supplanted by Wittgenstein (his *History of Western Philosophy* is currently a best seller but in Wittgenstein's circle they're probably wrinkling their noses at that). He is an admirer of *The Open Society* and on Popper's side. At some point Wittgenstein picks up the poker ...

"If the story refuses to lie down that's presumably because it's still not certain what happened next. Did Wittgenstein literally threaten Popper with the poker? (Popper never claimed that he did.) Did this David vanquish this Goliath with his quip about an example of a moral principle being that one ought not to threaten a visiting lecturer with a poker? Did Wittgenstein throw down the poker and storm out, or put it down and go quietly?

"For me, the recent controversy was valuable in eliciting, at five minutes to midnight, recollections from people who were there; but most of these questions are still unresolved."

Meanwhile, we are happy to fan the fires of the debate a little further with a remark by one of Popper's former colleagues at the LSE: "Popper was a notorious liar". Discuss.

Sci-Phi

1: The open future

Mathew Iredale

The future is open, alterable, to some extent malleable by us. The past is closed, unalterable, part of the irrevocable record of history.

                                                            J R Lucas

We have all had the feeling, at some time or other, that we didn't need to do what we did. Crossing the road, choosing a sandwich, phoning a friend, we feel that we could easily have not crossed the road, chosen a different sandwich or not phoned the friend. We've had the strong feeling, really known, that if we were to magically find ourselves in exactly the same situation again that we could have made a different decision.

Otherwise, why do we apologise when some of our decisions turn out to be hurtful to others; why do we punish or praise people for their actions; why do we differentiate between those who are forced into making their decisions and those who are not? It must surely be because we share with J R Lucas the feeling that the future is open to us, much of the time, and to some extent malleable by us. But what if this feeling is an illusion? What if the future is closed, unalterable, and not at all malleable by us?

This problem has concerned philosophers for centuries, usually as one part of the enduring debate over the nature of free will, and it has often seemed as if it is a problem without a solution. Indeed, I do not propose to offer a solution here (if only) but rather I wish to suggest that any future attempt at a solution must fully consider the startling implications of Einstein's theory of relativity if it is to be taken seriously.

It is generally agreed by physicists that one of the consequences of the theory of relativity is that we should abandon the common sense view of reality as being composed of three dimensions of space and a clearly distinct fourth dimension of time in favour of the view that reality is actually composed of four dimensional spacetime. This view of reality has some profound implications for our understanding of time. For we have to accept that we are no longer dealing with a three dimensional reality evolving in time. Rather, according to the physicist Russell Stannard, we have to accept:

> ...that our 4-D spacetime cannot evolve in time because time is not something separate from it: time is incorporated into the spacetime itself.

This faces us with one of the most curious features of spacetime: it never changes; it just sits there – doing nothing. All of space is there – but so too is all of time.

Just imagine: the whole of time – what we call the past, the present and the future – it is all there. Every instant of time is there on an equal footing with every other instant. On an equal footing. I mean that.

The whole idea of an absolute past, consisting of fixed events that used to exist but do so no more, and an absolute future, consisting of uncertain events that do not yet exist - all this is entirely foreign to the notion of a four-dimensional existence. I repeat: according to Relativity theory, all of time exists. (p48)

This same position is also described by the well known physicist Paul Davies:

In the [theory of relativity] there is no universal present, and the entire past and future of the universe are regarded as existing in an indivisible whole. The world is four dimensional (three of space, one of time), and all events are simply there: the future does not "happen" or "unfold". (p137)

His conclusion goes to the very heart of our feelings about ourselves and the way in which we view the world. It seems to deny that which we feel we know to be true: that the future is open. But before we are too quick to reject this extraordinary conclusion we should ask ourselves: is all that is being denied anything more than a feeling? And if not, then should we not base our beliefs, whatever they are, on something more substantial than that? For even though our feelings can tell us a great deal, they can also easily fool us. We can hallucinate, for example, or be hypnotised, and so come to believe things that are simply not true. In the end, we surely have to admit that we have never actually known that the future is open, we have only ever felt that it is. Consequently, when faced with apparently sound scientific evidence to the contrary, we need to do some very careful thinking indeed, if we are to reach a satisfactory solution to such an enduring and enticing problem.

Python, Parrots and Positivists

Gary Hardcastle

One benefit of being a professional philosopher (aside from listing "professional philosopher" as one's profession on forms) is that you can do almost anything you like. Thus some time ago I holed up with the collected works of Monty Python. I emerged, bleary-eyed, convinced of something long suspected: Monty Python is this century's greatest expositor of analytic philosophy.

How could this be? First a bit of history. Analytic philosophy has spent the last seventy years engaged in two successive revolts. If you hadn't noticed, don't feel bad. Philosophers engaged in revolt look exactly like philosophers not engaged in revolt. To find philosophical revolt you go to the philosophical journals. That's where you find our first revolt, the revolt against metaphysics. This occurred in the 1920s-30s and was carried out by the Logical Positivists, now regarded in some circles as demigods and in others as Neanderthals capable of giddiness over the casting of Mahler's 3rd Symphony into first-order predicate calculus. That aside, the Positivists' revolt against metaphysics was really successful. It was so successful that even now, when everyone agrees that Positivism is dead, and that even if it isn't dead its arguments against metaphysics (to use a technical expression) suck pond water, metaphysics courses throughout the analytic world still begin with earnest hand-wringing over whether or not it's now finally okay to study metaphysics.

The irony is that the Positivists, whose basic complaint against metaphysics was that it was irretrievably confused and fuzzy, themselves had a notion of metaphysics that was, well, confused and fuzzy. The fuzziness was manifested in a couple of technical glitches in the Positivist program. Whenever anyone came up with a means of sorting out the good philosophy from the metaphysical, some upstart logic whiz would point out that the proposed means either ruled out some clearly good philosophy or ruled in some ghastly bit of metaphysics. Even worse, nobody could find an acceptable way to defend the main weapon in the Positivist's arsenal, the verifiability criterion. The verifiability criterion said that the meaning of a meaningful statement was conveyed completely by the way in which it was verified. The criterion was enormously useful in accomplishing an end-run around metaphysics; since metaphysical statements couldn't be verified, the criterion told you they were meaningless. Things went swimmingly until someone realised that the verifiability criterion *itself* couldn't be verified. To verify it, you'd have to sort out all the meaningful statements beforehand, and that you couldn't do without first assuming the verifiability criterion! So the verifiability criterion was not verifiable. If it's not verifiable, then, according to itself, it's meaningless. So the verifiability criterion might as well be metaphysics.

What does all this have to do with Monty Python? Well, it's now clear that the Positivists weren't revolting against metaphysics *per se*, but against philosophy itself. Really, they were upset that philosophy had not made progress when other sciences had. It seemed like philosophy had somehow forgotten to keep in touch with the real world. Instead it spiralled off into bizarre realms where you could say anything at all and get away with it because there was no way to determine the truth of what you said or indeed if you even really said anything at all in the first place. This is really the first, and the biggest, theme of contemporary analytic philosophy – the contempt for philosophers of yore who managed to get nothing done while everyone else was off figuring out neat stuff like natural selection or gravity.

Now take the Monty Python short, "International Football". In it we have a football match with a twist: it's Germany versus Greece, with *philosophers* playing. Hegel, Marx, Heidegger, Jaspers, and Kant for Germany; and Heraclitus, Plato, Socrates, and Aristotle, among others, for Greece. At the start of the game they all suddenly ... pace the field in whisker-rubbing thought, ignoring the ball. The commentators follow the action, such as it is. With minutes to go, though, Archimedes has an idea. "Eureka!" he shouts, kicking the ball and initiating a drive to the German goal. Socrates heads it in for a Greek victory, 1-0.

Notice a few things. First, not one of the players is a Positivist. That's because all the Positivists are in the stands, screaming "Kick the ball, you nits!" if they're at the game at all. There is Wittgenstein, but you can tell by the tweed that it's Wittgenstein of the *Philosophical Investigations*, reviled by Russell for having abandoned good (i.e., analytic) philosophy. It's not even a philosopher who starts the ball rolling, so to speak, but Archimedes, an engineer. All the others just wander around – wasn't it annoying? Well, the Positivists were annoyed too, and that's why they revolted.

Back to the verifiability criterion. Despite its troubles, the verifiability criterion became the cornerstone of verificationism, the position that the only way to say something meaningful is to say something that can, in principle, be determined to be either true or false. Part of verificationism is the notion that for each statement about the world there is a set of experiences that by itself determines the truth value of that statement. This is *semantic reductionism* about statements. If you're out to verify "The cat is on the mat", for example, then presumably you're looking for certain experiences, like *seeing* the cat on the mat. Experiencing that guaranteed the truth of the statement; at least that's what verificationism told you. But reductionism couldn't be true. To determine the truth or falsity of a statement you need not only the right experiences, but the truth or falsity of other different statements too. Verifying that the cat is on the mat is not a matter of experience alone, but of verifying other statements also, like 'Light rays travel in straight lines' or 'I am not having another flashback.'

Now, if you admit that language gets its meaning by being hooked up with the world, then the failure of semantic reductionism means that sentences do not have meanings all by themselves but only when they hang out with other sentences. Quine put this well in 1951: 'Statements about the external world,' he wrote, 'face the tribunal of experience not individually but only as a corporate body.' This is *semantic holism.*

As far as philosophical positions go, semantic holism is great fun. It says you can't really assert a meaningful statement without implicitly asserting other statements – indeed, perhaps your entire language – simultaneously. It also allows you to rationally hold any arbitrarily chosen statement as true no matter what evidence is presented against it, so long as you adjust your convictions elsewhere. So, if you want to maintain the cat is on the mat when everybody else denies it, you can do so by holding that atmospheric phenomena are making it look like there's no cat, or that the cat on the mat is a transparent cat, and so on. And you can maintain *these* claims by making still further adjustments in *other* claims. This sounds like silliness, but it is just the kind of silliness the Positivists had hoped to do away with.

Now we turn to the beloved "Dead Parrot Sketch". Here we have Mr. Praline, returning a caged parrot to the pet shop where he recently bought it. His complaint? The parrot is dead, and was dead when he bought it. Indeed, he discovered upon arriving home that it had been nailed to its perch. The shopkeeper is unconvinced: the parrot is sleeping. When Mr. Praline pulls the parrot and tosses it to the ground, it falls with a thud. Now it's stunned, the shopkeeper insists. As far as the nailing goes, the parrot has to be nailed to its perch, for otherwise it "would muscle up to the bars and ... Vroooom!"

Mr. Praline is the verificationist. He verifies the state of the parrot by *seeing* it dead, *watching* it fall to the ground, *finding* it nailed to its perch, and so on. The shopkeeper is our more sophisticated holist. He knows that maintaining the truth of statements concerning the bird's fatigue or strength will allow him to maintain that the parrot is alive. You'll notice that the shopkeeper is never brought to accept that the parrot is dead.

The second revolt in contemporary analytic philosophy is the revolt against Positivism, of course, led, not surprisingly, by the post-positivists. There are some commonalities between the two. Like the positivists, post-positivists typically believe that understanding anything really important, like how we know, what there is, or what's right and wrong, means first understanding our language, which is the means by which we express what we know, what there is, and what's right and wrong. Throw in semantic holism and it should come as no surprise that the story of analytic philosophy since the fall of Positivism is the story of successive and somewhat uncoordinated attempts to sort out the consequences of the fact that the unit of meaning in a language is not the sentence but the language itself.

Good thing too, because semantic holism threatens society's very foundation. Holism seems to warrant bad reasoning, for it allows one rationally to maintain any statement come what may. That's bad enough. But it took about a half-second for analytic philosophers to realise that things were, potentially, much worse. Philosophers in the analytic tradition have long believed deeply that, one way or another, reason was society's foundation. Trying to be of use, philosophers have come up with theories of how reason works, such that it can be integrated into daily life. But, as students of logic often notice, theories of argument often ask that you grant certain statements, like "a sentence can't both be true and false at the same time", beforehand, *without argument*. But if holism is true, we can't count on our fellow citizens to accept these starting points. Nor can we expect to convince them that they ought to accept them if they don't! In short, if holism is true, then the whole notion of argument, and of reason, is up for grabs.

Now find, and watch, "The Argument Clinic". Here, for £5, you get an argument. Our protagonist's session begins when his host, Mr. Vibrating, claims that he already announced that this was the right room for an argument. "No, you haven't," responds our protagonist. "Yes I did," comes the response. "You didn't!" "I did!" "You didn't!!" In time our hero objects that what he's getting is not an argument. "Argument is an intellectual process," he says. "Contradiction is just the automatic gainsaying of any statement the other person makes." The predictable response: "No it isn't." With no common ground, their conversation devolves to hysteria. It's funny stuff. But on some accounts it's a glimpse of the end of civilisation.

Not all post-Positivists were so imbued with this apocalyptic vision. Indeed, some were unimpressed by the news that rationality could not be the foundation of society, they having already decided that rationality was overrated. We'd been managing well so far without much of it, after all. What grabbed these folk was that semantic holism suggested that it took only a small difference in linguistic behaviour to warrant the conclusion that two people were speaking different languages. If you also suspect that a speaker's language determines that speaker's world, then perhaps each of us literally has our own world, wildly different than our neighbours'.

Now have a look at the sketch, "Nudge Nudge". Two men share a drink at a pub. One plies the other with innuendoes, the answers to which he understands as further innuendoes, encouraging yet *further* innuendoes. "Aaaaaaaah bet she does, I bet she does, say no more, say no more, knowwhatahmean, nudge nudge?" climaxes one exchange. For the philosophical uninitiated this is a comedy of miscommunication, but for the semantic holist, who suspects that the slight linguistic differences between these two might make for different worlds altogether, it is a tantalising bird's-eye-view glimpse of the human predicament.

I trust you, the reader, are convinced at this point – Monty Python *is* this century's greatest expositor of analytic philosophy. Oh, there may be grumbles – after all, nothing has been said about either existentialism or the history of philosophy. Rest assured, Monty Python has covered both, the former in their wonderful take on the Myth of Sisyphus, "The Cheese Shop", and the latter in the ditty without which no philosopher's training is complete, the "Bruces' Philosophers Song", also known as "The Australian Philosopher's Drinking Song". You can peruse both in your time on the WWW. I, on the other hand, plan to return to Kant, albeit with a stack of *Flying Circus* episodes and one finger on the play button – to illuminate the passages I don't quite understand.

Burning questions

Why have the Germanic countries produced so many great philosophers and Mediterranean ones so few?

Basil Redhead

In true philosophical fashion, I question the question. There is a confusion of categories in it. "Germanic" (ethnic/linguistic) is contrasted with "Mediterranean" (geographic). This confusion is most apparent in the case of France, which a) has its capital in northern Europe and b) has a decent haul of great philosophers; but on the other hand i) has a Mediterranean coast and ii) is traditionally regarded as a Catholic country. I suspect that the answer (once the question has been logically tidied up) is that philosophy requires a wealthy society and is provoked by social and intellectual change. Here insert history of modern Europe.

Brendan Larvor

A forteriori – philosophy is Greek not only by etymology and Greece is a Mediterranean country! Besides the large number of Greek philosophers there have been many Arabic philosophers from the Middle East, another Mediterranean region – without whom incidentally the ancients' work would have fallen victim to an over-zealous clergy. France too is a Mediterranean country and I suggest he doesn't make such implicit statements in France! May I also suggest Basil Redhead visit a good library and look at the philosophy section or alternatively have a look at *The Oxford Companion to Philosophy* by Honderich which will give an excellent overview on the various strands of philosophy. Just because some philosophers are more widely known than others doesn't make them any greater – fame is no guarantor for insight. Perhaps he meant to ask why the names of Germanic philosophers have greater currency today than those from Mediterranean countries *other* than Greece – to that an easy answer would be "politics" and a more complex one would require a PhD study – how about it Mr. Redhead, I'd love to read it!

Timothy Hilgenberg

Dietrich Bonhoeffer, the German theologian, had a theory that because of the pleasant climate the mediterranean actually produced more thinkers. Whereas because of the less pleasant climate, the Germanic peoples had produced more engineers!

Davuid Gallie

Paradoxes
4: The heap
Francis Moorcroft

So far we have only considered paradoxes that involve self-reference. *"This sentence* is false", "The set of all sets that does not contain *itself"*, "No-one knows *this proposition"*. It's now time to look at other kinds of paradox.

A man with 10,000 hairs on his head isn't bald and surely subtracting one hair from his head can't make a man who isn't bald into a bald man. So a man with 9,999 hairs on his head isn't bald and subtracting one hair from his head can't make a man who isn't bald into a bald man. So a man with 9,998 hairs on his head isn't bald ... So a man with 1 hair on his head isn't bald and subtracting one hair from his head can't make a man who isn't bald into a bald man. So a man with no hairs on his head is not bald.

To give a second example: 1 stone is not a heap of stones and adding one stone to what is not a heap cannot make it into a heap. So 2 stones are not a heap and adding a stone to what is not a heap cannot make it into heap. So 3 stones are not a heap ... So 9,999 stones are not a heap and adding another stone cannot make it into a heap. So 10,000 stones are not a heap.

Paradoxes of this form are known as *Sorites* and are credited to Eubulides. The title "Sorites" is actually a pun. In Greek it means "heap" and the second example above involves a heap; but also it stresses the form of argument that is involved: the argument relies on a step by step addition (or subtraction), which is a heap of premises, and asking the question, "when is something a heap – or bald – or not?"

To make this a little clearer, it may be worth saying more about what a paradox is, and stating the paradox more formally. A *paradox* can be defined as an argument which starts from premises which appear to be true and yet, after reasoning that looks valid, ends up with an apparently false conclusion. To put the second example above more formally, we have the premises

> 1 stone is not a heap of stones
> 2 stones are not a heap of stones
> 3 stones are not a heap of stones
> ...

and the conclusion

> Therefore, 10 000 stones are not a heap of stones.

So the premises appear to be true, the conclusion seems to follow validly from the premises (by reasoning that adding one stone to what is not a heap cannot form a heap) yet the conclusion is false – a paradox. As the conclusion cannot be accepted then either the premises must be shown to be false or the reasoning shown to be invalid. But which?

One way of resolving these paradoxes is to recognise that they involve vague concepts such as "bald" and "heap" and it is very difficult in certain situations to decide whether or not these words apply to a particular collection of stones or a particular person – such terms are difficult to apply in borderline cases. So maybe we should *either* precisely define what we mean by a heap *or* just accept that using vague concepts leads to incoherence and avoid using them.

The first option would involve giving a numerical value for what we mean by "a heap", that is stating exactly the value of n such that n stones aren't a heap but that n + 1 stones are a heap. But surely any such value would be arbitrary. The second option is tempting until we realise just how many concepts used in ordinary language are vague: for example, I am tall and my sister isn't, but what about my girlfriend, when her height is midway between the two? When do I have a long day at work, a late night, or a large meal? Certainly language contains some concepts that are not vague – such as "is 1.95 metres tall" or "worked for 10 hours and 47 minutes" – but when such a large amount of our concepts are vague we may start to worry that no-one ever understands what anyone else is talking about.

While recognising that there is a great deal of vagueness in language, it should be distinguished from other problematic aspects. The word "bank" for example, is not vague but ambiguous: It may apply to the side of a river or a financial institution, The word "game" is neither vague nor ambiguous but applies to a great many different activities by virtue of its generality. Such distinctions may be of use in assessing what counts as vagueness or not.

One final question: when we describe something as "vague" do we always have a clear idea of whether the concept applies or not? That is, is "vague" a vague concept or not...?

In Praise of Zeus

Robin Harwood

"But is there any good reason for believing in the ancient gods, Professor?" asked Amy, shifting her chewing gum from one side to the other. "Surely you are not going to suggest that we believe in them on the basis of faith?"

"Indeed not", I said. "After all, by faith you can believe in anything that takes your fancy, provided your powers of self-persuasion are strong enough. It is better to use reason to decide what to believe."

"Doesn't that mean that you have faith in reason?" asked Mark.

"It is a common suggestion that depending upon reason is equivalent to having faith in, say, the God of the Christians, but in fact there is a big difference. Faith in God is faith that something exists, that God is part of reality. Such trust as we have in reason is trust in a method for working out solutions to problems, such as the problem of what things are part of reality. Belief that an entity exists is quite different from believing that a particular method will lead to knowledge of reality. Trust in reason is a trust in a method of thinking, a method of acquiring knowledge. Belief in God is believing in the existence of something we think about, a thing to be known. Do you see the difference?"

They claimed that they did, and then Jeff asked "But still, isn't that just faith that reason works?"

"No, our belief in reason isn't faith. It is justified belief. It is based on the fact that it has proved itself better than other methods in the past. If we were to discover some other method that clearly was more successful than reason, in so far as it gave us all the knowledge that we can gain from reason and more besides, then we would be inclined to prefer that method to reason. Again, if reason were to be clearly shown to be a bad method, we would give it up. This attitude to reason is not faith. Religious Faith seems to be belief that is held without evidence, and perhaps even against reason, and in spite of all countervailing evidence. Or so it seems to me. Religious people say you should never give up faith, no matter what."

They nodded in agreement. I wondered briefly if Socrates' yes-men also were thinking about who it was who decided their final grade. Then Amy asked, "Okay. So if you don't believe in the ancient gods by faith, what reason do you have? Do you mean like Epicurus and religious experience? Visions of the gods?"

"Not that, no. Do you remember what William James said about non-evidential reasons for religious belief? We discussed it last week (*TPM1*). Well, I can provide a non-evidential reason for believing in the Gods. Roger Scruton has claimed that one of the foundations for morality is *pietas*, by which he means something like respect for the natural order. Mary Midgley has agreed with him, and I tend to agree too, on that point at least. Now the word *pietas* is the origin of our word piety, because the respect for the natural order involved respect for the ancient gods, who are gods of the natural world."

Melody then asked thoughtfully, "I thought you said they were something to do with various aspects of human life, Professor. Like, Apollo is the God of philosophy and science and stuff."

(I do like the way my American students call me "Professor".)

"Indeed, but Apollo is also connected with the Sun", I said (vaguely, because I could not remember exactly the connection between Apollo and Helios), "just as Artemis is a goddess of wild places but also the goddess of midwifery and childbirth. They form a link between human life and the natural order." I was making this bit up as I went along, but it sounded okay. Good enough for undergraduates, anyway.

"So you mean, Professor, that we should worship the old Gods to link ourselves with the natural order?"

"Exactly! And this not only makes you feel part of the natural world, and less alienated, it also increases your *pietas*, which makes you more moral. But there is more to it than that. If you honour the Gods, they may well choose to help you, and provide you with the good things of life in this life. Forget about the after life. If there is one, they might help you there as well, but this life is the one you know about. Get their help now. And remember, the Gods are famous for taking a dim view of those who do not honour them. They will at best ignore you, and may make things go badly for you. So it is best to be on the safe side and honour them."

Mark chewed his gum skeptically (with a 'k') for a moment, and then asked "What if they don't exist, Professor?"

"If they don't exist, then you have lost nothing (unless you are going to overdo it and sacrifice hecatombs of oxen) but you have still raised the level of your *pietas* by reverencing the natural order. We can formalize it as "Harwood's Wager".

"If the Gods exist, and you honour them, you get the spiritual benefits of feeling part of the natural world, and increased *pietas*, and you also have the chance of their help in this world, and perhaps the next as well. If the Gods exist, and you do not honour them, you get nothing, and may even be punished in this world or the next. If the Gods do not exist, and you honour them, you get the spiritual benefits, though not the help in this world. If the Gods do not exist, and you fail to honour them you get nothing.

"Clearly the best option, as a matter of sound practical reason is to honour the ancient gods. If we combine James' argument for the legitimacy of non-evidential belief with Pascal's Wager (suitably modified), we find they have provided us with a fine piece of pagan apologetic."

I have to report that next morning I found my students all worshipping the Sun with prayers and offerings of chewing gum.

Sci-Phi

2: The self

Mathew Iredale

Who are you? That is to say, what is it about you that makes you "you"?

At first glance, the answer to such a question seems obvious. You are the person who has your thoughts, your feelings, your beliefs and your memories. These are what make you who you are. They are what define your personal identity. No one else, not even your twin, if you had one, would have the exact combination of thoughts, feelings, beliefs and memories that you have. There is only one "you" in your head, as it were. This would seem to answer the question of who you are. Of course, one might want to ask, to obtain anything more than a basic answer, "just what are your thoughts, feelings, beliefs and memories?" and whilst the task of collating these thoughts, feelings, beliefs and memories may be a long and time consuming one, this would surely be a practical and not a theoretical problem. Wouldn't it? After all, there's only one "you" in there, isn't there? Well, possibly not. In fact, this common sense assertion seems far from certain when one considers the startling results of a series of psychological experiments carried out by Roger Sperry and Michael Gazzaniga from the 1960s onwards.

The experiments involved people who had suffered from serious epilepsy. It was found that the spread of this crippling condition could be lessened if the corpus callosum – that part of the brain which connects the left and right hemispheres of the brain – was divided surgically. The result of this, indeed, the whole reason for the surgery, is that the two hemispheres are then unable to communicate with each other. A bizare consequence of this is that, since one hemisphere only has control of one arm, and can only see what is in one half of the visual field, psychologists can present to this person two different written questions in the two halves of his visual field and can receive two different answers written by this person's two hands.

Derek Parfit has probably discussed the philosophical implications of Sperry & Gazzaniga's experiments in greater depth than anyone and has provided the following imaginary example to clearly illustrate their experiments. Imagine that the subject looks fixedly at the centre of a wide screen, whose left half is red and right half is blue. On each half in a darker shade are the words, "How many colours can you see?" With both hands the person writes, "Only one". The words are now changed to read, "Which is the only colour that you can see?"

With one of his hands the person writes "Red", with the other he writes "Blue".

From this result (and from Sperry and Gazzaniga's actual results) one can conclude that the subject has two streams of consciousness, in each of which he can only see one colour. In other words, the subject appears to be having two different series of thoughts and feelings.

But this raises a dilemma. For if, as I stated at the start, we wish to say that a person's identity is to be defined in terms of their own thoughts, feelings, etc. and we can demonstrate that a person can have two different series of thoughts and feelings, then should we hold that there are in fact two different individuals present, or rather that one cannot adequately define who one is in terms of the thoughts, feelings, etc. that one has?

It seems obvious immediately to conclude that there is clearly only one individual present, but that he has been forced to appear to be two by some rather underhand psychological manipulation. However, consider the following possibility. The same subject has his brain completely separated such that one half is put in one body and the other half in a separate body. Would we count these two subjects as still being only one individual? Well, why not? What, psychologically, has changed? Surely nothing: the subject's brain is no more divided psychologically then it was when both hemispheres were in the same skull. On the other hand, to view two completely separate thinking, feeling subjects as the same, and not as two individuals in their own right, seems ridiculous. When do the thoughts, feelings, etc. of the subject cease to be all his and become ... well, become what? His and "someone else's"? Or will "he" cease to exist and two new individuals be created? Whichever conclusion we come to it seems to completely undermine our common sense notion of personal identity, and perhaps that is where the problem lies.

I shall finish on that point, except to ask once again: "Who are you?" Not so obvious now, is it?

Meeting yourself

Michael LaBossiere

> A gust of air whirled round me as I opened the door, and from within came the sound of broken glass falling on the floor. The Time Traveller was not there. I seemed to see a ghostly, indistinct figure sitting in a whirling mass of black and brass for a moment – a figure so transparent that the bench behind with its sheets of drawings was absolutely distinct; but this phantasm vanished as I rubbed my eyes. The Time Machine had gone. Save for a subsiding stir of dust, the further end of the laboratory was empty.
>
> *The Time Machine, by H. G. Wells*

Travel, of any kind, involves journeying from one point to another point. In the case of spatial travel, this involves journeying from one location in space to another location. This sort of travelling happens all the time. For example, millions of people make the trip from the fridge to the couch each day. Time travel, being a form of travel, also involves journeying from one point to another. However, in the case of time travel, the journey is made from one point in time to another point in time. While it might seem an odd sort of thing to say, time travel is happening all the time. In fact, you are doing it right now. Even as you read this sentence you are travelling towards the future at the rate of sixty minutes per hour. Of course, that sort of time travel is not what most people find interesting. One of the more interesting types of time travel involves moving from the present time to the past. Another interesting type of time travel is going into some future time, without all that time consuming mucking about in all the time between now and then.

While it has been claimed that if a person travels far enough, she will end up back where she started, no one claims that if you travel far enough you will meet yourself. However, if time travel is possible, a person should be able to travel back in time and, in theory, meet herself in the past. If a person takes care not to travel too far ahead in time, he should be able to meet himself in the future.

Naturally, there are all sorts of problems and paradoxes involved with people travelling about in time to meet themselves. For example, suppose Bill, who is thirty four now, decides to go back in time and kill himself at age twenty. Obviously, if Bill succeeds in killing himself, he would not exist at age thirty four. Hence, he could hardly go back to kill himself. Yet, if Bill is able to travel through time, he should be able to go back and kill himself. These sorts of problems probably help fuel the sale of aspirin.

Fortunately, this article is not about those brain teasing paradoxes. For example, I will not argue whether Bill would be committing murder or suicide if he went back in time to kill himself. Instead, I will focus on the problem of simply going back in time and meeting yourself. Or your past self. Or however one would word it.

As has been noted above, if you can travel backwards in time, then you should be able to meet yourself. This creates an interesting metaphysical problem, that of explaining how the very same thing, namely you, can be in two places at exactly the same time.

In order for the same person to be in two different places at the same time, the components that make up the person would, of course, have to be capable of existing in more than one place at the same time. In other words, the components would have to be capable of multiple location.

Another philosophic problem, namely the problem of universals, also involves the issue of the same thing existing in different places at the same time. Very, very briefly, one part of the problem of universals is determining what it is for two tokens to be of the same type. To give a concrete example, part of the problem would be determining what it is for six different green objects to all be the same in respect to their colour. Two popular solutions to the problem of universals, as it relates to the possibility of entities existing in multiple locations at the same time, are as follows.

David Armstrong, a well known Australian philosopher, argues that there are instantiated universals (David Armstrong, *Universals*, Westview: Boulder,1989). Briefly, an instantiated universal is a property (such as *being green*)that can exist in multiple locations at the same time. Going back to the problem of universals, for six different objects to all be green would be for each object to instantiate the universal green. The very same, identical universal green would be wholly located at each green object. To be even more specific, if a frog and a leaf are the same shade of green, the green of the frog and the green of the leaf are one and the same entity which happens to be multiply located.

Now, suppose that any person is essentially a unique set of instantiated universals. (If, for example, a person is her soul, the soul would be composed of universals.) In this case it would seem that going back in time to meet yourself would be possible. What would make this possible? First, it has been assumed that what makes a person who he is, say Bill, is made up of universals. Second, a universal, as has been established, is capable of existing in distinct locations at the same time. Hence, the universals that make up the person Bill happens to be can exist in different places at the same time. So, it would be possible to have a person identical to Bill standing five feet from Bill. This identical person could be the Bill from the future. Since Bill and Bill from the future would be identical, then it would seem they would be the same person. Hence, if a person is composed of universals, then he could travel back in time to meet himself. It would simply be a case of the same person existing in different locations at the same time.

Keith Campbell and I, among others, reject instantiated universals in favour of tropes. Briefly, a trope is a property (such as *being green*) that can only exist in one location at one time. Trope theorists explain what it is for two tokens to be of the same type in terms of resemblance. As an example, for six different objects to all be green would be for each object to have its own distinct green trope. Each green trope would be a different entity from the other green tropes, but they would resemble each other and would all be taken to be green because of their resemblance.

Now, suppose that any person is essentially a unique set of tropes. In this case it would seem that going back in time to meet yourself would be impossible. What would make this impossible? First, it has been assumed that what makes a person who she is, say Sally, is made up of tropes. Second, a trope, as has been established, is incapable of existing in distinct locations at the same time. Hence, the tropes that make up Sally cannot exist in different places at the same time. So, it would not be possible to have a person identical to Sally, say the Sally from the future, standing five feet from her. Thus, if Keith Campbell and I are correct, it would seem that a person could not travel back in time and meet herself. This would also entail that time travel is not possible.

Since I am committed to tropes, but find the notion of time travel fascinating, it would be nice if there was a way to reconcile trope theory with time travel. Perhaps there is a way of doing this.

According to modern physics, which is based on Einstein's special theory of relativity, there is no such thing as absolute and universal time. Instead, time is seen as being relative to each thing. In this context, time is relative in the sense that each thing carries around its own personal time scale which does not, in general, agree with the time scale of other entities. The relativity of time is subject to empirical proof. For example, if one precision atomic clock is left on earth and another is placed into the American space shuttle, the clock in the shuttle orbiting the earth will lag behind the clock left on earth. The difference in time is due to the speed of the shuttle and its location in earth's gravity well. Given the fact that this experiment has been conducted, it is hard to deny the relativity of time.

Once relativity is established, the notion of same time goes out the window. Each thing has it own time scale which varies with its location and speed, so there simply is no objective basis upon which sameness of time can be grounded. In this case, nothing can be in two different locations at the same time. Roughly put, being in a different location would put it in a different time.

One effect of the relativity of time would seem to be the end of instantiated universals. This is because an instantiated universal has to exist in different places at the same time. Since there is no such thing as sameness of time, instantiated universals simply cannot exist as defined.

A second effect of the relativity of time is that it enables time travel to be reconciled with tropes. The way this happens is as follows.

It is contended that people can be made of tropes, yet still be able to travel back in time to meet themselves. For example, imagine that Bill has travelled back in time to ask himself where he left his keys. Bill tells future Bill where they are in return for a bit of advice on how to play the ponies later on. Both Bill and future Bill can be composed of identical tropes, yet still meet. This is possible because Bill and future Bill, like any other entities, will actually exist at different times. Hence, there is no need for Bill and future Bill to exist at the same time. They simply have to have their times "close enough" to allow them to interact. Thus, I can have my tropes and time travel, too.

WAS THE WALTZ A METAPHOR FOR HEGEL'S DIALECTIC?

OOM PA PA, OOM PA PA

SYNTHESIS

THESIS

ANTITHESIS

ACCORDING TO HIS SISTER HEGEL WAS A LOUSY DANCER...

.STAMP.

And I quote...

What they said about the Twentieth World Congress of Philosophy

So compartmentalised has the academic world become that the various Aristotelians, Marxists, Nietzscheans, Eco-feminists, set-theorists, Logicians, Ethics-wallahs, philosophers of biology, neo-Kantians, philosophers of physics, even philosophers of sport, spent little time talking to those who were not of their own ilk. In this *fin-de-siècle* Babel, the few exchanges that did take place were dialogues of the deaf.

Tunku Varadarajan in The Times 15/8/98

Dressed in saris and shorts, bow ties and berets, more than 3,000 philosophers from around the world have converged on two swanky downtown Boston hotels for the 20th World Congress of Philosophers in the largest such gathering in history.
[...] Despite the gathering's lofty topics, the philosopher's are not above consumerism (World Congress of Philosophy Key Rings at $2.00 are a big seller), partying (a cash bar and live jazz band were organised for Monday night's reception) or rudeness (a crowded elevator of philosophers neglected to make room for a priest).

The Washington Post 16/8/98

More than 3,000 philosophers heard the call to service, but also got a harsh critique from their host, Boston University Chancellor John Silber, who said they have themselves to blame for their isolation. Silber charged that feminists, Marxists and others had turned philosophy into "an assault on reason." [...]
Silber's main target, feminists, replied that Silber had caricatured their efforts to combat sexism, which they said was a common tactic to put women down.

The Boston Globe 11/8/98

When 3,500 individuals professionally devoted to this proposition ["dare to think"] are gathered under one roof, as happened at the 20th World Congress of Philosophy in Boston this week, the effect may be more of Babel than of 18th-century discourse. Modern philosophy speaks a bewildering variety of languages, from analytic logic to existentialism, poststructuralism, semiotics and the wilder shores of ecofeminism, and there is a fair degree of apartheid between is practitioners.

The Times leader 15/8/99

Coffee, anyone?

The media go to the cafés philosophiques

The room settled on "laughter and philosophy", as suggested by an earnest young woman in the corner. "Laughter is an act very ephemeral," she intoned, "and yet charged with meaning, whereas philosophy is austere and there is a paradox, I think." She said this quite unsmilingly. [...]

After an hour, the conversation had moved no further than the point that "laughter exists on many levels". It was time for some food.

Bee Wilson says it all about cafés philosophiques. The New Statesman 11/9/98

Before heading off, I asked a friend who has an MA in philosophy for some tips. He advised me to open every speech with either "It depends what you mean by..." or "Yes, but in an important sense, no". On arrival, I found about 12 people gathered around a table passing a mic from hand to hand like a joint. A bloke in specs and a jumper was arguing that science now explained everything and that it was time for it to look inside mankind and discover what it could about the soul. This outraged a man with a soft Irish accent, who complained that science was too reductive and argued for a return to the mystical. A chap with a crop was outraged, and challenged him to define mysticism's qualities, which the mystic refused to do.

Stephen Armstrong The Observer Life 21/2/99

London now has a Café Philosophique of its own, organised by the French Institute, plus a new Anglo-Saxon equivalent: "Pub Philosophy". The brainstorm of philosophy doctorate student Bryn Williams, this takes place on alternate Tuesdays at Costa Coffee in Soho [...] "A lot of people think philosophy has nothing to do with the real world," says Williams. "They just don't have any idea of what it is. But thinking is a bit like washing up. It takes motivation but once you start it's easy."

Helen Kirwan-Taylor, FT Weekend 27/3/99

Le café philosophique est arrivé

Joseph Chandler

The Anglo-Saxon attitude towards the French has always been ambivalent, in philosophy as in all things. We praise the way in which philosophy is an integral part of everybody's education, lament that the only way to get philosophy into our bars is to tie it in with football and envy the level of celebrity French intellectuals enjoy. And yet French philosophy itself is often held in contempt as a woolly, pretentious, meaningless, willingly obscure practice for which the name "academic discipline" is a terrible misnomer.

It was with a heightened sense of this ambivalence that I tried out the new *Café Philosophique*, run by the Institute Français in affluent Kensington this winter. The idea was to import one of the jewels in popular French culture's crown to London, and hopefully kick start the movement in the UK. The *Café Philosophiques* are extremely popular in France. Meeting regularly in, as the name suggests, cafés and bars, the idea is that, with the help of a qualified mediator, participants engage in philosophical discussion on a theme of their choosing.

There was a certain buzz of excitement among the generally middle-class, middle-aged mass that filled the institute the day I went to check it out. The Institute's café was certainly stylish and with smells of fresh *café au lait* and pastries filling the air, the feeling that one was in a haven of civilisation was irresistible. I was genuinely looking forward to the discussion.

Our mediator this session (and for all the Institute's current programme) was Gayle Prawda, who regularly hosts such groups at Paris' famous *Café de Flores*. Dr Prawda informed us that she would take suggestions for topics from the floor and then we would choose which one we wanted to discuss. The suggestions came thick and fast. "Is this a community?" "Is thought an addiction and love the cure?" "What is rationality?" "There is no such thing as a philosophical problem". Questions were bandied around, frequently with a cavalier disregard for coherence or precision. One question, "Can we go beyond the animal body?" was restated by Dr Prawda as "Can we go beyond the animal instinct" as if this were simply a clearer synonym. Eventually, in a demonstration of Murphy's law of shopping, having heard numerous alternatives, Dr Prawda announced she would go for the second suggestion, "What is normal? What is objectivity?"

But before I could get over my horror at this absurd conflation of two quite distinct questions, the event took a farcical turn. First, a man in the crowd protested that the event had been "hijacked". Having been promised a vote, the convenor had now chosen the topic herself! After a short debate on the merits of such a course of action, a vote was held on which voting system to use, and then there was a show of hands for each one of the suggested questions. (Our protester was clearly acting on no less a motive than principle – he voted for the question Dr Prawda had chosen.)

So, after twenty-five minutes, the discussion could finally begin. It soon became clear that a large number of the contributions fell into one of two categories: Profound sounding but unhelpful rhetorical questions (such as "What are we searching for anyway?" "Normal for whom?") and unsupported assertions of a subjectivist or relativist nature (such as "There are no facts because all facts require interpretation.") There was also a fair smattering of unfunny jokes. These generally involved selecting a word from the last speaker's last sentence – such as "milk" – and swiftly asking, "What's milk anyway?" For some inexplicable reason, this would always get a good laugh. This raised the intriguing possibility that most people there didn't take what was being said seriously anyway, and that it was all a kind of pointless parlour game.

There were some glimmers of sense. After half an hour someone objected that the statement "there is no objective truth", which most participants seemed to endorse explicitly or implicitly, entails a paradox and is perhaps self-defeating, as if it is true, then there is at least one statement which is objectively true, namely itself. This would mean it was not true. Secondly, he attacked the supposition that ethical relativism (the belief that there are no objective moral values) entails absolute moral tolerance. Another speaker pointed out that the discussion had failed to distinguish between the statistical and value-laden senses of normality. But none of these fruitful observations were taken up by the discussion and we soon reverted to the seemingly endless game of verbal pass the parcel.

My notebook soon began to fill with outraged rants, which in retrospect, were a little harsh, such as "They're jumping from question to question with (apparently) no genuine desire to seek out answers," and "The discussion is rambling and unstructured. A tiresome round of pseudo-intellectual opinionating."

This was not what I had hoped for. There's little enough philosophy in popular culture without what little there is being dismissed out of hand, so I spoke to Gayle Prawda after the discussion was over to hear her side of the story. Press comments from the first session had generally been quite critical. So Dr Prawda was pleased to be able to put her side of the story. First off, as this was my sole experience of the *Café Philosophique*, maybe this wasn't typical? Alas, it was.

"Today we dealt with the subject pretty well," thought Dr Prawda. "Last time I felt we were getting off the subject, but the subject was a lot more difficult." (Is it better not to have been born?)

Trying not to think too much about what this last session must have been like, I put some of the objections to her. Firstly, the accusation that what happens at a *Café Philosophique* is that you get a stream of people expressing their opinions and there's never really a chance to focus in on them, and make progress. It's just an exchange of platitudes.

"There are some inherent problems because of the spontaneity of the way in which it is presented. Obviously, you're not going to have the structure that you would have in a conference or a class. We don't know the subject that we're going to be discussing in advance, we don't know who's going to say what. Now there is a moment where you're able to pull the ideas together and try and synthesise them in a way that they move on for the future, and that's the ideal situation you want to get to. But sometimes, even when you do the synthesising, the participants may not necessarily pick up on it. They have their own things to say or they're still responding to someone who spoke half an hour ago. That's why I think it shouldn't be judged just on was it is – there are a lot of ramifications that it has outside of the two hours that occur. The first two hours people are either listening and taking in or giving out. Afterwards they're either circling off into their own little groups, still thinking about it or discussing it, and, if they have ways of writing or incorporating some of this it goes beyond what we can see in the first two hours."

"You have to have a series [of meetings], because then indirectly or directly they start to pick up some of the tools or skills that philosophy has to offer, that is, how to think, how to analyse, how to examine, how to question, to question your questions. All of these methods that will help you to examine your own life."

Such a view of philosophy as a teacher of thinking skills has recently become quite popular. But I put it to Dr Prawda that some people would say that if you take the overall effect of the *Café Philosophique*, it may reinforce some of the negative ideas people have about philosophy, that it is just about expressing your opinion or saying things which sound profound but don't necessarily have any content to them. People aren't challenged that often on what they've said.

She admits that the debate element can get "scanned over" and replaced by a simple exchange of views. "It depends on the subject and the group involved how the dynamics go."

Ever helpful as I am, I try to offer a line of defence. In French culture, isn't it the case that philosophy is understood in a broader sense than it is in Anglo-Saxon culture? For example, Bernard Henri-Levy is known as a philosopher in France, whereas we'd think of him more as an "intellectual" than a philosopher as such. So maybe Anglo-Saxon critics of the *Café Philosophique* are simply missing the point?

"Well, you have to know what distinction you're making. An intellectual is a very well read or cultivated person who can use their intellect in various different situations. A philosopher is someone who's asking basic questions about life and existence. A philosopher is a bit more rigorous. He tries to use various methods to get close to the truth and to try to clear away all of the clouds that are clouding the way to that truth that he's trying to get to."

But, I insist, isn't there something about the *Café Philosophique* format which undermines that rigour?

"Well, what is the relationship between the *Café Philosophique* and the role of the philosopher? We're going back to the Athenian times where Socrates was shouting out and discussing things out in public areas. This is making philosophy more accessible to people, to everybody, and to make people more accessible to philosophy. It's reviving philosophy. Rather than it become that old, absolute, intangible, obscure, inaccessible language, let's talk to the people about these ideas."

The analogy with Athens is interesting, I reply, but surely the major difference is that Socrates went out and spoke to people and listened to their opinions, but then he always followed up on them and questioned them. Socrates didn't just go and listen to the people and comment from time to time.

"That's one of the disadvantages of a large group," replies Dr Prawda. "But when you have a small group of twenty people meeting regularly, you have the time and the place to be able to sit down and say, 'Now what made you think that?' The size of the group determines the outcome or the form of the discussion."

So is one the aims of the *Café Philosophique* to encourage the proliferation of more smaller groups?

"Definitely. It's not necessarily a question of competition. The more the merrier. I do feel there is a need. I'm always amazed, but the place I'm in in Paris, there's never enough room. It's always full. I'm already drawing eighty to a hundred people. I think people are attracted to the idea of looking at things philosophically, which was always kept in this ivory glass tower."

The cafés are certainly proving to be popular, and Dr Prawda is surely right to say that we shouldn't judge their value solely on what goes on in the meetings, but also on their effect afterwards. Nonetheless, I was not the only one with reservations. One participant, whose probing questions clearly marked him out as someone with a background in the subject, was Peter Cave of Imperial College. After the meeting, he lamented, "It's very sad that some glaring errors were just left hovering." Sad indeed, for with so few opportunities for the non-academic public to participate in philosophy, surely they deserve some rigour when the opportunity is presented to them.

Paradoxes
5: Zeno's paradoxes (1)
Francis Moorcroft

The four Paradoxes of Zeno, which attempt to show that motion is impossible, are most conveniently treated as two pairs of paradoxes. The reasons for this will hopefully become clearer later. The first two paradoxes are as follows.

The *Racecourse* or *Stadium* argues that an athlete in a race will never be able to start. The reason for this is that before the runner can complete the whole course they have to complete half the course; and before they can complete half the course they have to complete a quarter; and before they can complete a quarter they have to complete an eighth; and so on. Therefore the runner has to complete an infinite amount of events in a finite amount of time – assuming that the race is to be run in a finite amount of time. As it is impossible to do an infinite amount of things in a finite amount of time, the race can never be started and so motion is impossible!

The second paradox is that of Achilles and the Tortoise, where in a race, Achilles gives the Tortoise a head start. The argument attempts to show that even though Achilles runs faster than the Tortoise, he will never catch her. The argument is as follows: when Achilles reaches the point at which the Tortoise started, the Tortoise is no longer there, having advanced some distance; when Achilles arrives at the point where the Tortoise was when Achilles arrived at the point where the Tortoise started, the Tortoise is no longer there, having advanced some distance; and so on. Hence Achilles can never catch the Tortoise, no matter how much faster he may run!

The diagram below may help to understand this argument.

The race starts at t0 with the Tortoise having a head start over Achilles. By time t1, when Achilles has reached the point at which the tortoise started, the tortoise has moved on; by t2 Achilles has reached

the point where the tortoise was at t1 but the tortoise has moved on; by t3 Achilles has reached the point where the tortoise was at t2 but the tortoise has moved on; and so on. To be sure, the distance between Achilles and the tortoise is getting less and less each time but Achilles never catches up with – far less overtakes – the Tortoise.

Zeno, it seems, believed quite seriously that motion did not exist and that arguments such as these established it. What do we, who believe that races can be run and slow objects can be overtaken by faster moving ones, say in response?

One common reply is that Zeno has misunderstood the nature of infinity. Modern mathematics, it is said, has shown that the infinite sequences that Zeno generates do have a finite sum. In particular, to take the Racecourse example, the sequence $1/2 + 1/4 + 1/8 + 1/16 + \dots$ is equal to 1.

This reply, however, misunderstands what modern mathematics has shown. Mathematicians do use sequences such as $1/2 + 1/4 + 1/8 + 1/16 + \dots$ but they say that they have a *limit* of 1, or *tend to* 1. That is, we can get nearer and nearer towards 1 by adding on more and more members of the sequence, but not actually arrive at 1 – this would be impossible because we are considering an infinite sequence. So far from providing an argument against Zeno, mathematics is actually agreeing with him!

Further, this reply seems to miss the point of Zeno's argument: simply pointing out that there is a branch of mathematics that deals with the infinite does not reduce the puzzling aspects of the Paradoxes. We *know* that races can be run and that Achilles will overtake the Tortoise, what we want to know is what is wrong with the arguments that show that these things can't happen.

The first two Paradoxes of Zeno attempt to find contradictions in the idea that motion is *continuous* and space can be infinitely subdivided. But motion may not be continuous: space may be *discrete* and motion be a series of tiny jumps. On this view there would be a finite – but very large – number of steps between the beginning of the race and its end. So the Paradox of the Racecourse could be avoided by saying that there is some first, incredibly small, step that can be taken, where there is no step of half the size. Similarly, there is some small, and indivisible, last step that Achilles can take which will allow him to catch the Tortoise and then overtake her. This possibility is criticised by the other two Paradoxes of Zeno to be considered next time.

Burning questions

Who was the Greek philosopher who lived his life in a barrel and what he was doing there?

Mr F Nielsen, Colorado, USA

Diogenes, the best known of the Cynics and a pupil of Antisthenes, reputedly lived in a barrel and owned nothing but a cloak, a stick, and a bread bag. The reason for this was the Cynics' emphasis that true happiness is not found in material things.

Submitted by email

It was not exactly a barrel. He lived in a pithos – a large wine jar, normally made of clay. According to Diogenes Laertius he took up this abode because the real estate agent whom he had asked to obtain a small house for him prolonged the search beyond his patience. Given that Cynics made a virtue of living on no more than nature required, he may have been making a point about genuine need as contrasted with vanity and desire. Since people were sometimes buried in pithoi, his point might even have been that we need no larger habitation when alive than we do when dead.

James Dye

Is there a philosophy of horticulture?

Jessica Rutherford

Early work by Frank Zappa explored the possibilities inherent in the human/vegetable interface. Check albums such as *Freak Out* and *Absolutely Free*. In particular I recommend the short musical essay, *Call Any Vegetable*. That aside I often find myself becoming deeply reflective in the garden. I watched a caterpillar endlessly circling the rim of a bucket. Occasionally it would stretch searchingly into the emptiness of the bucket and then think better of such a radical move. It continued to circle. "Us" I thought. That said, there is a "Green" movement around with political parties, pressure groups etc. that has the occasional thing to say about issues horticultural.

Nigel Marshall

And I quote...

From The Philosophers' Magazine

I think [women] have got more common sense on the whole than men and found it rather boring to go on and on and on about theoretical cases that did get rather ludicrous. Certainly in Oxford there was a school of philosophy which in a sense was realist because it thought you could just look at the world and see what things were right and wrong, but the sort of examples that those people took were all of the most trivial kind. I'm particularly thinking of A. J. Pritchard, who was a very influential philosopher in Oxford just before the war and whose books on moral philosophy were full of questions like whether you had a right to family news, whether you had fulfilled your duty by posting the letter or only if the letter had been received at the other end and went on and on about setting yourself to post the letter. I think people like Phillipa Foot got fed up with it and thought, "Well, let's look at what really happens," and that was a very good move.

Baroness Mary Warnock, TPM7

I do think that women are less likely to be prepared to spend their time playing games in philosophy and that's what I think a great deal of philosophy is doing. Some of it, obviously, is simply complicated but it's pretty far from life. I don't think that it's that women can't perform these formal operations, but they wish for some reason to be shown why they should. That's certainly my situation – I can't speak for women in general. If you're doing philosophy at all, if you're engaged in the way that ideas work, then it's a male peculiarity to wish to go right up in the air and go round in circles without relating them to anything else.

Mary Midgley, TPM7

By now, few philosophers believe that conceptual analysis can be entirely divorced from empirical fact. But none, I think, would hold that normative political philosophy can be divorced from empirical fact. We have to know the facts in order to know what is possible and practicable. We also have to know the facts even to get the right questions onto the table. For example, if we do not know that women get beaten up and malnourished in their homes, we might forget to ask questions about distributive justice in the family — as so many male political philosophers have forgotten over the ages.

Martha Nussbaum, TPM5

Sport for thought

Simon Eassom

The discussion of play, games and sport by philosophers is not new. Plato placed great emphasis on the training of the body as a fundamental part of the education of the infamous "philosopher-kings". In Eastern philosophy, the body and mind come together through martial arts such as karate and tae-kwon-do. A slew of continental philosophers, in modern times, have used play and sports as exemplars of particularly human activities or as metaphors for their distinctive world views. However, in most cases, philosophers have simply used games and sports to illustrate otherwise independent ideas and arguments. Alan Wertheimer, in his recent book *Exploitation*, goes a little further and devotes a whole chapter to college sport in the USA as a perfect example of the kind of real-life practice in which exploitation occurs. It is largely here, in the area of applied philosophy and ethics, that the philosophical interest in sport has come into its own.

Over the last thirty years a distinctive literature has grown up around the philosophical study of sport. Its content has been quite diverse, reflecting the backgrounds of its main contributors. In the USA, the renowned philosopher Paul Weiss published *Sport: A Philosophic Inquiry* in 1969. More generally, the main publications came from academics with eclectic backgrounds working in areas such as kinesiology (loosely translated as sports studies), human movement studies, and the anthropology of play and leisure that represented the emerging interest through the 50s, 60s, and 70s in the study of sport from all perspectives, social and scientific. Typically, such works as Eleanor Metheny's *Movement and Meaning* (1968) and Howard Slusher's *Man, Sport and Existence* (1969) represent early (and sometimes quite crude) attempts to develop unifying theories of mind and body or existential meaning through sport and exercise.

In the UK, an interest in sport among philosophers has emerged slightly differently. Most of the literature has been directly related to Physical Education and its authors are largely professional philosophers of education. One of their favourite topics for ongoing discussion has been the morality or otherwise of competition, particularly in the context of education. Here, physical education and sport have been taken as exemplars of activities that are inherently competitive, by definition. Does this make them immoral? Additionally, the Wittgensteinian philosopher David Best in his work on aesthetics has heavily influenced aesthetic education, dance education, and educational gymnastics.

It would be reasonable to say that in the formative years, the 60s and 70s, sport philosophers borrowed from mainstream philosophy and synthesised the ideas of numerous "big names" into a coherent philosophical commentary *on* sport, rather than a legitimate "philosophy *of* sport". Essays abound on subjects such as the rejection of mind-body dualism from the experiential perspective of performance in sport and dance; the use of competitive sport as a tool of moral education; Kantian denunciations of cheating; Marxist critiques of the excesses of commercialised sport; Sartrean eulogies on sporting solitude, existential meaning, and authentic living. All of these early discussions have the flavour of being mainstream philosophy *applied* to the study of sport. But does sport have anything to say to philosophy?

One topic that has focussed the attention of most of the profession and typically reflects the neuroses of any fledgling discipline has been the foundational one of establishing exactly what phenomena we are talking about here: What is sport? What are games? At times these discussions, as is usual in all such areas, have dissolved into picayune squabbles about necessary and sufficient criteria for calling activity "x" a game or sport.

The starting point for such analysis has often been a provocative and fascinating book by the Dutch historian and anthropologist, Johan Huizinga, called *Homo Ludens: A Study of the Play Element in Culture,* first published in 1938. Huizinga presents the thesis that human beings have evolved as the animals that play games and that this unique feature, as much as any other, has driven the emergence of civilisation.

The approaches taken to the question "what is sport?" have generally mirrored discussions elsewhere on topics such as the theory of art. There is one exception among these discussions that has stood the test of time and become something of a "bible" for sport philosophy initiates. The Canadian philosopher Bernard Suits published numerous articles in the 1960s and 70s on the definitional problem of "game-playing", and his collected thoughts were published in 1978 in neo-Socratic dialogue form under the curious title, *The Grasshopper: Games, Life, and Utopia.* Based on the fable of the grasshopper and the ant, Suits develops a thesis that the good life, by logical necessity of the goal of life being the reduction of all instrumental action to non-instrumental action, is ultimately one spent playing games. The Grasshopper is a Christ-like prophet whose vision of utopia is debated and discussed by two mixed-up disciples who angst over the transition from being long-lived worker ants to being one-summer-only hedonist grasshoppers. It is a beautifully illustrated book, whimsical and witty, although, at times, slightly tedious. It is also, undoubtedly, brilliant. There is no better example in modern philosophy of Socratic dialogue used so effectively to develop a cogent thesis through argument and counter-argument.

Suits' *Grasshopper* marks a watershed in the sport philosophy literature. Identity crisis over, a more mature discipline emerges in the 1980s and 90s with a greater confidence that the study of sport does indeed have something unique to offer mainstream philosophy. For example, given the shift in moral philosophy away from the dry analysis of what Bernard Williams called "thin" ethical concepts (abstract terms such as good, bad, right, wrong) to descriptive, contextual, "thick" concepts (such as cruelty, honour, justice), any discussion of morally evaluative terms like "fairness" must necessarily involve the study of those contexts in which fairness is relevant. There are hardly more appropriate settings in which to discuss fair play than sport. In other words, to study such evaluative terms as cruelty or fairness is precisely to study the contexts in which such concepts are used: the cruel treatment of animals by sport hunters; the inherent formal equality and regulative mechanisms of rule-bound games. A discussion on the morality of "cheating" is in no way better served than by discussion of the highly complex assessments of acceptable and unacceptable practice in game-playing and sport. Such a discussion reveals that purely analytical definitions regarding intentional rule-breaking and deceit don't go far enough to account for the emotive use of such moral brow-beaters as calling somebody a cheat. A much deeper understanding of *ethos* and culture is required to make sense of them.

Sport provides a rich playground for a whole host of debates on the consistency of our moral judgements. How can we continue to justify the sport of boxing where violence is promoted by paying huge sums of money to modern-day gladiators? How can we legitimise the intentional infliction of serious physical harm by one person on another, or on an animal, for no other reason than entertainment? Where do the notions of freedom and consent fit in here? And paternalistic intervention? Nowhere are our racist and sexist assumptions more explicit than in our simplistic generalisations about black athletic superiority and female athletic inferiority, and through our tacit discrimination in favour of intelligent white strategists in key positions and black "workers" as full-backs, wingers, and out-fielders. Only in sport can violence and verbal abuse, which would be illegal on the street, be wholly within the law. What is aggression? Is it inherently immoral? And why is it only tolerated in sport and warfare? What's the difference between rules of a game and the rule of law? Games illustrate perfectly the frustrating tautology of rule-following: the first rule of any game is necessarily that you must follow the rules.

One has to look no further than the modern Olympic Games, or the soccer World Cup, to witness the significance of sport in everyday life. A discussion of whether or not Maradonna's "hand of God" or

Ben Johnson's drug-tarnished 100m world record were immoral acts reveals a great deal about the relationships between moral theory, moral judgement, and moral psychology in practice. The recent public debates in Britain about the banning of stag hunting with hounds and fox hunting bring utilitarian and deontological arguments to the fore in ways that are immediately accessible and recognisable as philosophical argument doing real work in real situations. These topics are just as worthy of the validating hand of philosophical treatment as abortion and euthanasia. Whilst the use of genetic engineering in medicine for enhancement of the human being is being blocked, athletes are already tampering with their biochemistry, altering their hormonal levels, experimenting with synthetic blood and slowly creating their own sinister agenda for the perfectibility of the human body. But sport doesn't matter, so they say ... it's just a game!

Sport philosophers who tackle these issues represent a healthy diversity of philosophical commitments. In their work you will find commentary on a diverse range of current, mainstream writers. However, you will find that it isn't just a serve and volley game. Sport philosophers genuinely believe that the study of sport has something worthwhile to offer philosophy, and thus keep the ball rallying back and forth a little longer, and certainly make it a more interesting game.

Sci-Phi

3: Reason
Mathew Iredale

> Reason: the power of comprehending, inferring, or
> thinking especially in orderly rational ways.
>
> *Webster's Dictionary*

If there is one ability that philosophers require above all else it is
the ability to reason. We pride ourselves on the fact that in philosophy
our arguments and our conclusions are based upon a reasoned study
of the available evidence. If we reject Descartes' dualism we do so
because we believe that we have reasonable grounds to do so: that
there are various philosophical and scientific arguments that make
dualism unattractive. We would be silly to reject it because we don't
much like Frenchmen, or because we object to the fact that Descartes
stayed in bed until midday (not an objection, admittedly, that many
undergraduates of philosophy would raise).

Although we may sometimes wonder how our peers can hold some
of their more idiosyncratic views, we still strive to present our objections to those views as reasonably as possible. And we expect to receive the same courtesy in return. No matter how much they may
want to, generally speaking philosophers do not laugh mockingly at
each other when engaging in debate. (We may threaten each other
with pokers, but that's another story.) We recognise that the views of
our peers have invariably been reached after years of reading, discussing and, most of all, thinking. We have come to our philosophical
beliefs through such reasoning and we believe the same to be true of
others.

But what if we are mistaken? What if we are not nearly as reasonable in our thought processes as we like to believe? What if we only
appear to be using reason in our arguments when in fact we are not?
Consider the following experiment described by psychologists R
Nisbett. & L Ross in their book *Human Interference: Strategies and Short-
comings of Social Judgement*. It appears to demonstrate that experimenters can prompt significant shifts in the attitudes of subjects unbe-
known to them. Here is Nisbett and Ross's own description of the
experiment:

> ..subjects are induced by the experimenter to give a talk or
> write an essay that is inconsistent with their private beliefs. In
> "sufficient justification" conditions, subjects are given large
> monetary incentives for such behaviour and consequently at-

tribute their compliance to the incentive rather than to any corresponding private belief. In "insufficient justification" conditions, by contrast, subjects are paid little or nothing for their counter attitudinal action, and, noting no salient external factors sufficient to account for their actions, and wrongly assuming that those actions must therefore reflect corresponding private beliefs, they change their attitudes so as to bring them in line with their behaviour. These subjects thus commit the fundamental attribution error. Had they correctly identified the situational cause of their behaviour, that is, the subtle social pressures to comply exerted by the experimenter and the experimental context, they would have had no reason to change, or even to reassess, their private beliefs.

The dilemma that this experiment raises is whether the insufficient justification subjects come to change their minds through reasonable argument or not. On the one hand, there appears to be nothing to prevent the subjects from exercising their ability to reason. They are not being forced to change their views by drugs or bribery or being fed misinformation by the experimenters. On the other hand such a wanton change of view by the subjects simply because they had to write an essay inconsistent with their private beliefs appears to be anything but reasonable. If we can change someone's view just by getting them to write an attitude discrepant essay for small or no reward it seems to indicate a distinct lack of reason in their thinking. It seems to indicate that they have given little thought to the reasons behind their beliefs and are as swayed by an opposing view as a blade of grass is by the wind.

Of course, it may be the case that each of the subjects came to change their views only after carefully considering the merits of the opposing viewpoint, something which they may never have had to do before they wrote the essay. If so, then the experiment gives no cause for concern. However, although this may indeed be the case, the fact that the experimenters apparently knew that they would be able to change the views of the subjects who received little or no payment somewhat weakens the argument. One would think, if reasoned argument had occurred, that some of the people would change their minds, some would not, and some would be undecided. One would not think that the subjects would all change their minds *and* that the experimenters would know this in advance.

There is, I suppose, one obvious way to settle the problem. Decide whether you think that the subjects acted reasonably or unreasonably in their change of view and then write an essay opposing your conclusion. Then see if you change your mind. Or better still, try it on a friend. But remember, don't pay him.

70

Bizarre News

The Pope has issued a "challenge [to] philosophy to recover and develop its own full dignity." The challenge comes in his latest encyclical, *Fides et Ratio* (Faith and Reason), which criticises philosophy for "abandoning the investigation of being" and having "concentrated instead upon human knowing", which "has given rise to different forms of scepticism and relativism".

Philosophy is also accused of neglecting four fundamental questions of perennial concern: "Who am I? Where have I come from and where am I going?" Why is there evil? What is there after this life?"

Although the Pope talks of "the rightful autonomy" of philosophy, the Pope clearly believes that, done rightly, philosophy will support the church. For example, he writes, "The church considers philosophy an indispensable help for a deeper understanding of faith and for communicating the truth of the Gospel to those who do not know it." This supporting role is also intimated in the statement that "there exists a knowledge which is peculiar to faith, surpassing the knowledge proper to human reason."

The Pope was once a Professor of moral theology and thus has some philosophical background. His approach is often considered to be Thomist, following the thought of Thomas Aquinas, whose thought merits its own section in the encyclical. The medieval feel is strengthened by the referencing of Anselm and Augustine with no more than passing acknowledgement to a few more recent thinkers the Pope admires, such as John Henry Newman, Antonio Rosmini and Edith Stein.

From the news pages of TPM5

Are we just extraordinarily immature or does anyone else find the acronym for the conference *Processes of Evolution in Real and Virtual Systems* at Krakow, Poland, amusing? The conference is calling itself "PERVS 98".

From the news pages of TPM4

And I quote...

[Peter] Singer's principle is that animals deserve the same consideration as human beings, where their interests are similar.

[...] how well does he live up to the demands of non-speciesism? Is he guilty of speciesist language? "I would prefer not to call people pigs in a derogatory way because that's unfair to pigs and fosters an image of pigs which is derogatory.

"But," he adds, "I once called someone spineless." Will the great kingdom of invertebrates ever forgive the professor for this slur?

Boris Johnson, Daily Telegraph 29/5/98

Having been teaching ethics for a very long time in British Universities as a philosopher, I'm struck how little reference is ever made to the terrible things that have happened in the 20th Century. Ethics ought to be rooted in some idea of the way in which human nature can go wrong and produce these disasters.

Jonathan Glover, interviewed by James Meek,
The Guardian 13/10/99

Long before children can be expected to take in the economic consequences of theft from supermarkets they must be taught to *want* to be good rather than bad, to develop an inner sense of what it would be shameful to do.

Mary Warnock, Prospect October 1999

Anthony O'Hear is a philosopher who has come to despair of reason. He styles himself a reactionary rather than a conservative, because after a survey of the thought of the past 200 years, he can find nothing worth conserving.

Bill Saunders, reviewing O'Hear's new book, After Progress,
Independent on Sunday 17/10/99

Foucault, a pessimistic post-Nietzschean, believing all is power, would probably think that a petty transgression like shoplifting was a blow against the internal hegemony of the power structure – just as he somehow may have convinced himself that not telling his lovers he was H.I.V. positive was a truly liberating act.

Ron Rosenbaum, revealing that Foucault is one of the most stolen
authors from Barnes and Noble, Union Square,
New York Observer 27/9/99

Hank and Heidegger

Simon Walter

I was intrigued by the promotional material that accompanied the first edition of *The Philosophers' Magazine* through the post. A handbill that sought to entice potential readers by espousing authentic yet accessible philosophy in contrast to an inferior form of *Pop philosophy* represented by the thoughts of Ted Nugent, rock singer.

To be fair, Ted, not normally considered a reticent and self-effacing man, has never claimed to have any intellectual pedigree. The one time leader of the Amboy Dukes, whose only hit record during the late sixties, *Journey To the Centre of Your Mind,* expressed less a precocious interest in phenomenology, and more a sense of juvenile dementia brought on by the fashionable narcotic abandonment of the times. Nevertheless, the ferocious empiricism explicit in the quote attributed to him – "I don't really think about deep things. If you can take a bite out of it, its real" – read like a refutation of *Idealism* reminiscent of Dr. Johnson's spat with Bishop Berkeley.

Why should we be surprised by the unintentional profundity of the remark? For pop music has always aspired to philosophical respectability. One calls to mind Sam Phillips, record producer and owner of *Sun Studios Memphis,* the Bethlehem of Rock'n'Roll, declaring that Charlie Feathers, a contemporary of the young Elvis and still recording today, was the, "Only abstract thinker to come out of Rockabilly music." He was working on six different versions of *Roll Over Beethoven* simultaneously. However, his reflections were purely formal. His preoccupation was with the conventions and limitations of the genre.

The same could be said of the mysterious *Oblique Strategies* of pop's original egghead and serial collaborator, Brian Eno. Devised with artist Peter Schmidt, these strategies were a set of *oracle cards* which predicated the lines of development in the musical composition. This pop aesthetics is an inevitable consequence of the self awareness that comes with the maturity of the medium. It is only when pop music has "something to say" about states of affairs in the world that it becomes truly embarrassing to listen to. From protest songs to charity singles, the list of pop crimes is too numerous to be included here because very few are innocent. But singled out for special condemnation must be the *concept album,* that uniquely pretentious artefact of the early seventies which could draw on any subject to tenuously link a bagatelle of songs.

In this company Ted Nugent is a pillar of wisdom because his observation, as an example of fortuitous ontology, not only throws into relief pop's tendency to take itself too seriously, but also serves to demonstrate that the distinction between *appearance* and *reality* is cardinal to defining what is and is not philosophy. Indeed, it is the very same contrariety that Plato drew upon when differentiating dialectics from sophism. It could be said that philosophy as a discipline begins with, and receives its impetuous from, the disparity between an intuitive sense that, how things appear to be is not necessarily how they really are.

Pop musicians, too, are often characterised as sharing the philosopher's critical attitude toward accepted wisdom of the day. However, by doing this they follow the precedent not of political thinkers like Plato, but rather those romantic artists of the mid-nineteenth century whose conception of *Bohemia* was first and foremost a privileged position on the metaphorical outskirts of current moral practice sustained by economic independence. This enabled the malcontent to pass judgement on society without getting embroiled in its everyday worries and concerns. Of course one could argue that the financial autonomy and tax exile status of the pop star are the proper credentials for social commentary. For it is only through detachment that contemplation is possible.

However, the pop music industry, with its Knights and Dames, is far more conservative than its audience and thus its frequent declarations on behalf of the downtrodden and the disenfranchised often seem disingenuous. This is mainly due to the ideology implicit in pop's commodity form. The *message* of the music is always compromised by the medium through which it is experienced and consumed. Pop's primary colours are novelty, spontaneity and spectacle. These qualities are not derived from the immediate demands of the musical material itself, but rather they are imposed from without by the necessity of the disposable form of the infinitely reproducible product. Although records may seem superficially different, all are marketed and sold in the same ruthless manner. Everything is dispensable except the excessive profit margin. One only has to think of the bewildering turn-over of black artists, due to the lack of long term investment in their careers, to realise that this leisure industry is capitalism in its most extreme form.

Hence, any philosophical reflection evident in the words of the song is reduced to the rank of a "gimmick", a way of establishing brand identity in a volatile market. All content is mere *appearance,* gesture without substance. There is no *reality* to be differentiated from the superficial.

No doubt an objection could be raised against this cantankerous position. Sartre in the novel *Nausea* makes a virtue of the paradoxical relation of commodity form and musical content. Listening to a recording of a black woman singing a Blues, the narrator finds, through his reflections on time, necessity and chance, that music experienced through the agency of the "sapphire needle" is uncannily enhanced;

"If I love that beautiful voice, it is above all because ... it is the event which so many notes have prepared so far in advance, dying so that it might be born. How strange it is, how moving, that this hardness should be so fragile. Nothing can interrupt it but anything can break it." The music becomes ethereal and a means of transcendence; "It filled the room with its metallic transparency, crushing our wretched time against the walls. I am *in* the music."

It may be the case that the music that emerged from the church and folk traditions of the persecuted retains an ability to elevate the listener simply because these pioneers could never be entirely assimilated into a commodity culture. It is the incongruity between the anonymity of the manufactured product and the intimacy of the human voice that asserts the indestructibility of the human spirit in a nihilistic age. Something *real* endures despite.

But maybe I am demanding too much. Maybe the authenticity I seek is merely a consequence of a conventional way of thinking about philosophy and its relation to the world. Martin Heidegger believed that Plato was missing the point entirely when he sought *Being* beyond ordinary devalued sense perception. Following Nietzsche he refused to give credence to a metaphysical duality of *appearance* and *reality*. Plato's desire for transcendental answers obscured the true nature of existence. From this perspective the only genuine philosophical question is "Why are there *essents* rather than nothing?"

If this is so, then one can have no serious objections to a medium that flaunts its lack of significance. It would seem churlish to criticise pop for not aspiring to greater profundity when its objective is to distract us from proper philosophical inquiry. Yet who in the history of popular music has asked the questions that Heidegger asks? Very few. Possibly Hank Williams. From Mount Olive, Alabama, he recorded *Lost Highway* in the late forties, its very title demonstrating an intuitive grasp of the meaning of the work of art as described in Heidegger's essay of the same period, *What Are Poets For?* In Heidegger's thinking, art is one of the pathways by which *Being* is encountered. *Being's* significance is historical. It is the ground and destiny of a people – "The unity of men, gods, earth and sky." In the 'destitute time" of the modern age the people have turned away from *Being* and are heading unwittingly towards the abyss. For only traces remain of the original pathway. It is the purpose of the poet to sense these "tracks of the old gods" and to sing a song of lamentation. The poet sings in the hope of turning the people around, back towards a possible reconciliation with *Being*.

For Hank Williams the *Lost Highway* marks not only the singer's disorientation in a disenchanted world – *"I'm a rolling stone, all alone and lost"* - but also the quest for an authentic way back to an intimacy with *Being*. In this case *Being* is the destiny of the American people, whose turning away towards the abyss is symbolized by the infidelity of a loved one. This is simultaneously revealed (pathway) and concealed (turning away) in the language of mythologized *Old West*. Only traces remain of what once was and *"With a deck of cards and a jug of wine"* the singer laments his destitution. The *"Road of sin"* is a metaphor for his fallen state and *"Sorrow bound"* he is cast out of society. As a moral outlaw his *"Rambling"* nomadic life becomes archetypical of the destiny of the American people in such nihilistic times.

In the final verse Hank addresses the *"Boys"* warns them of his fate – *"Take my advice or you'll curse the day, you started rolling down the lost highway."* Or as Heidegger would have it, "Poets are the mortals who, singing earnestly of the wine god, sense the trace of the fugitive gods, stay on the god's tracks, and so trace for their kindred mortals the way toward the turning."

Hank Williams died before he was thirty. Sensing his nemesis he penned that most sublime of epitaphs – *"I'll Never Get Out of this World Alive"* – and took his place among the seraphim of country music heaven.

Paradoxes
6: Zeno's paradoxes (2)
Francis Moorcroft

Last time we looked at the first two Paradoxes of Zeno, that attempted to show that if space is continuous and infinitely divisible then motion is impossible. This time we will consider the other two Paradoxes that attempt to show that motion is impossible if space is discrete.

What would it mean to say that space is discrete? It certainly doesn't *look* as if things move in jerky little jumps. An analogy could be made with motion picture film: each separate frame is a still photograph, but when it is shown at a rate of 24 frames per second it looks as if the motion is continuous. So perhaps space could be like this, with only a finite number of states possible. Zeno's Paradoxes are intended to show that this possibility also leads to contradictions, so that if we accept the conclusion of the first two Paradoxes – that motion is impossible if space is continuous - then Zeno will have established that motion is impossible *whatever* space is like.

The third Paradox is the *Arrow*. Consider the path of an arrow in flight: at each instant of its path the arrow occupies some position in space – this is what it means to say that space is discrete. But to occupy some position in space is to be at *rest*. So throughout the entire path of the arrow through space it is in fact at rest!

The fourth Paradox, the *Moving Blocks*, is the hardest to follow. Here we have three rows of blocks of uniform size and an equal distance apart. One row is at rest, the second row moves past the first row in one direction, the third row moves past the second row in the oppo-

Position 1

A1 A2 A3
   <<< B1 B2 B3
C1 C2 C3 >>>

Position 2

A1 A2 A3
B1 B2 B3
C1 C2 C3

site direction. Both rows move at the same speed. We need only consider three blocks in each row and what must happen in the change from Position 1 to Position 2 in the diagram above.

For this change to happen, B1 and B2 and C3 and C2 each have to pass one member of the stationary row. But in the same time B1 and B2 will have passed two members of the C row and C3 and C2 will have passed two members of the B row. As the motion is uniform, it takes the Bs and Cs an equal amount of time to pass a given object. But the problem is that they pass two objects in the time it takes to pass only one.

This argument seems the least impressive of the four as it treats the Bs and Cs as if they are in motion when they pass each other but at rest when they are themselves being passed. However, the problem is deeper than this. Consider what would happen if the members of each row were as near to each other as they could possibly be, i.e., they occupy adjacent points in space, and that the change from position 1 to position 2 takes place in the smallest amount of time – an instant. Neither of these assumptions seem problematic. Now in the first instant C3 is opposite B1 and the next instant it is opposite B3. When did it get to pass B2? There is no time when this could have happened!

So time, it seems cannot come in instants and space cannot be discrete. We are left with the option that time and space must be continuous – but that was the assumption that was criticized by the first two Paradoxes. In fact the Arrow is deeper than it first appears as the flight of the arrow would be equally impossible even if space and time were continuous as the arrow would, in effect, have to be at rest an infinite amount of times during its flight. Thus, whether space is continuous or whether it is discrete, motion is impossible.

So you're saying
Hannibal Lecter wasn't evil
– just hungry

Bizarre news

The seventh running of one of the world's bizarrest sounding competitions is set to take place in Bulgaria in May 1999. The International Philosophy Olympiad, previously an almost exclusively eastern European affair, is set to widen its reach, with the USA sending a team, and the UK possibly also entering for the first time.

But what is a philosophy olympiad? Images of the famous Monty Python philosophy football match should be banished at once. A jury meets the morning before the competition and sets four or five topics, which are either philosophical problems or quotations from philosophers. Competitors then have four hours to write an essay on one of the topics. The jury – invited philosophers from the competing nations – then mark the essays according to knowledge of the history of philosophy, originality, skill of argumentation and the correct use of language.

As Professor Havas, one of the organisers explains, "There seems to be a misconception about the IPO. It is a competition not for philosophers, but for high school students, selected in each participating country by means of a competition conducted by, usually, a panel or jury of teachers of philosophy."

The aims of the competition are to "encourage creative thinking and enquiry among students, by showing the values inherent in intellectual efforts; to stimulate intellectual competition; and to promote philosophical reflection about science and ethical reflection on the problems of modern world."

From The news pages of TPM5

And I quote...

An apparently widely-held position in the philosophy of science is what is known as the "underdermination of theories". This states that any given body of data will always be compatible with a number of mutually incompatible theories, and so one cannot use observations in order to chose any particular theory. When I challenge the philosophers to provide me with just one other explanation for how genes code for proteins, or the composition of water, or the circulation of the bood, they become uncharacteristically silent or claim I do not understand. On this latter point, they are certainly correct.

Biologist Leiws Wolpert, Independent on Sunday 17/1/99

There are lots of lousy ways to start studying philosophy and students intrigued by the subject should beware of them. Reflecting on the lyrics of a Bear of Very Little Brain, and the superficial insight they give into one of philosophy's deepest thinkers, may only be the most obviously hopeless.

Stuart Jeffries on why to avoid Pooh And The Philosophers (along with Philosophy Made Simple and Wittgenstein in 60 Minutes)

Novelists don't age as quickly as philosophers, who often face professional senility in their late twenties.

Martin Amis

If you want to think about the future, reading an academic book is the last thing you do.

Sadie Plant, so called "Cyberfeminist", author of Zeros and Ones and PhD in Philosophy, on why she has turned her back on academia.

For the last 200 years there has been great philosophical creativity taking place within academic institutions, practised by figures such as Hegel and Heidegger. It seems to me that that age is at an end. At the moment, the imperatives of academic life are determined by the fact that everything you teach has to be examined, everything you write has to be assessed as a contribution to research. It militates against the kind of systematic diffidence and self-questioning which seems to me to be essential to philosophy and was certainly there at the time of Socrates.

Jonathan Rée, Nightwaves, BBC Radio 3 21/9/99

The Best and The Worst Philosophers

It's official – Aristotle is the world's favourite philosopher, while the thinker most thought of as overrated is Jacques Derrida, an international icon of cultural studies.

Over the last few months, *TPM* has been taking votes over the internet and at philosophy conferences to try and find out whose contributions to philosophy are most and least valued. From the day voting opened it was clear Aristotle was going to win, though his 12% of votes cast was ultimately only 2% higher than Plato. The Ancient Greek one-two was followed by Kant, meaning that the most important contributions to philosophy are seen to have been made prior to two hundred years ago.

In keeping with this view, all the top three most overrated philosophers produced their greatest works in the last 150 years. The most interesting case here is Nietzsche. Although he received 6.5% of votes for the most overrated philosopher in history, he actually received a higher number and percentage of votes in the poll for the most significant (7%), but didn't make the top three. This apparent paradox is explained by the fact that there was more agreement about the significant contributions than about the overrated ones, which meant you needed a lower number of votes to top the latter poll than the former. Nietzsche therefore deserves the epithet the philosopher philosophers most sharply disagree on.

The poll perhaps reflects the anglophone bias of the respondents. The web, from which most votes were culled, is largely an English-language medium, and "continental" philosophy is notoriously sniffed at by Anglo-Saxon philosophers. The consistent pattern of the voting does suggest the poll is an accurate reflection of their tastes.

Poll Results

Which philosopher has contributed the most to the advancement of human understanding?

    1. Aristotle   2. Plato   3. Kant

Which philosopher's contribution to the subject has been most overrated?

    1. Derrida   2. Marx   3. Nietzsche

860 voters

News, TPM5

Analysis
(TPM6)

What started as a short news item in *The Philosophers' Magazine* and ended up featuring prominently in *The Guardian, The Independent on Sunday, The Daily Telegraph*, BBC Radio Four, the BBC World Service and even on BBC Television's News24? The somewhat surprising answer is that it was our poll to find the philosophers whose contributions to the subject have been most valuable, and most overrated. Now that the media frenzy has died down, it's possible to consider a little more calmly just what, if anything, the significance of the poll really is and what the reaction to it tells us about the place of philosophy in contemporary society.

To start off, we need to go right back to when the exercise was conceived. What was the point in *TPM* conducting the poll? It certainly wasn't to find out who the best and worst philosophers really were. We had two motivations. Firstly, we were not aware of any similar poll having been carried out before. We thought it would be an interesting exercise to see who people with a real interest in the subject (as all the voters were) rated. In particular, we wanted to see whether the "greats" really were as well-thought of as was presumed. We would also be able to test the received wisdom that continental philosophy is held in disdain by the Anglo-Saxon world. On this front, there seems to have been a sea-change in attitudes over recent years. Where once there were two competing camps not talking to each other, it no longer seems outrageous to talk of Derrida in the same breath as Dewey, or Nietzsche alongside Nagel. The poll would allow us to find a rough and ready measure of how far this *rapprochement* had come.

Secondly, such ranking exercises are always a bit of fun, and if they get people talking about philosophy who otherwise wouldn't be, then it's fun in a good cause. And talk they did, as newspapers, radio and TV not only mentioned the poll, but also gave room for discussion of it. Radio Four's *Today* programme invited Professor Emeritus Ted Honderich and Alan Montefiore, founder of the Forum for European Philosophy to talk about it in their daily discussion slot. *The Guardian* made it the subject of an editorial. News24 got Brian Hanrahan to interview the editor about it in its *Europe Direct* programme. And when a week later the *New Statesman* made Alain de Botton's essay about the enduring appeal of the ancients in philosophy its cover story, even though he made no mention of the poll, one would be justified in suspecting that this was no coincidence.

But what did the poll show? In raw terms, it showed that in the English-speaking philosophical community, the philosophers most people thought had made the greatest contributions were, in order, Aristotle, Plato and Kant. And the philosophers deemed most overrated were Derrida, Marx and Nietzsche. The latter is a special case. He polled more or less the same number of votes in both the greatest contribution and most overrated categories, making him the philosopher people most violently disagree about. As someone who once advocated philosophising with a hammer, one can sense he might have been quite pleased about that.

These results seem to have three worrying implications. Firstly, people believe the most important contributions to philosophy were made prior to two hundred years ago, and mostly two thousand years ago, while the most overrated philosophers had done their work in the last 150 years. It's all grist to the mill of those who think philosophy is a dead subject. Secondly, the Anglo-Saxon/continental divide seems to be holding up pretty well, despite the apparent entente of recent years. Thirdly, where are the women?

Honderich expressed his dismay at the first of these implications. "There is something very bizarre about that poll turning up ancient philosophers at the top. Ancient philosophy is the past of philosophy and it ought to be sloughed off, like science sloughs off its past. Philosophy should start in the 17th century with Hobbes."

But on reflection, the result may not necessarily suggest an obsession with our past. It has to be remembered that the question was about the "greatest contribution". It is often the founding fathers of any discipline who are most able to make the greatest contributions to it. Think of Aristotle, who virtually single-handedly invented several branches of philosophy, plus a few humanities, social sciences and sciences on the side. It just isn't possible to do that kind of thing any more. The greatest of today's minds are lucky to found a single school of philosophy, let alone a branch of it.

Another consideration on this point is that it is the very nature of polls to find the lowest common denominator. It's rather like the pop music charts. The number one single is the one that appeals to the widest range of people. It may well be the favourite song of none of them. We allowed people two votes and we suspect that many people voted for one person they really believed had made the most valuable contribution and one whom they felt couldn't really be left out because they are such towering figures in the history of our subject. As there is more agreement about the latter, they poll more votes. So perhaps we should not be so worried about our ties to the past after all.

What of the second indication – that the divide between Anglo-Saxon and continental philosophy is still a very wide one? Honderich and Montefiore's discussion suggested this may not be a real concern. Both agreed that the two traditions are almost like two different subjects. As Honderich put it, "One thinks of French philosophy that it aspires to the condition of literature or the condition of art, and that English and American philosophy aspires to the condition of science." And in case you wondered which side he was on, he couldn't resist adding, "French philosophy, one thinks of picking up an idea and running with it, possibly into a nearby brick wall or over a local cliff," though he admitted that "five million frogs can't be wrong."

While it might be true that the two traditions are quite different, Honderich's playful asides echo more serious criticisms tossed in the direction of mainland Europe. It's not just that people think of the disciplines as different, there is clearly also a good deal of animosity. Remember, people considered the continentals overrated. This is not the judgement of a community that sees the continental tradition as different but equal. It is also surprising that when interdisciplinary studies are becoming more and more *de rigueur*, the difference between Anglo-Saxon and continental philosophy is held up as a justification for not paying much attention to, or even dismissing, the latter. If there can be dialogue between different subjects, surely there can be dialogue between two traditions within the one subject?

The final note of concern is the absence of any women philosophers on either list. Is this a sign that philosophy is misogynous? It is difficult to reach a firm conclusion here, but it is probably fair to say that the poll only reveals the historical fact that, for many reasons, it has been much harder for woman to join the academy than it has been for men. We would have to look for the importance placed on women philosophers today to discover whether philosophy is misogynous. This poll only reveals what is true of all academic disciplines – that for centuries women were marginalised. Whether that is still the case is neither demonstrated nor disproved by the poll.

But perhaps the most interesting part of the whole exercise was the media's reaction to it. It certainly shows that, despite what many think, there is a great deal of interest in philosophy in society at large. However, the media didn't quite know how to treat the subject. Most approached it with that air of amused embarrassment so typical of the British when they try to deal with intellectual matters. News24 in particular went for the jocular angle, putting the discussion in the traditionally light "and finally" slot. But despite this, the coverage was not generally flippant. *The Guardian's* editorial pretty much summed up the feeling. It started unpromisingly: "What is the point of philosophy? Obviously, its first purpose is to supply jokes for the rest of us." But having got the obligatory British snigger out of the way, it went on to reveal a genuine concern for the place of philosophy in our society. It criticised the "terrible insularity" of anglophone philosophy and said, "We should strive to build intellectual bridges with the rest of Europe rather than retreating further into the austerities of much recent anglophone philosophising."

So our poll ended up provoking an impassioned plea by a national broadsheet newspaper for a greater international role for Anglo-Saxon philosophy. That has got to have made it all worthwhile.

Paradoxes
7: Self-deception
Francis Moorcroft

When I deceive you then I know the truth about something and you don't; what's more, I deliberately try to conceal the truth from you, telling you lies if necessary. That is, I try to get you to believe something that I know to be false. So deception is a matter of: I know something, you don't; I hide the truth from you. But with this understanding of deception, how is *self-deception* possible? Do I have to know the truth about something and then, simultaneously, hide the truth from *myself*? How could this be? How do I *know* the truth and yet tell myself that it isn't the truth?

Yet self-deception is more than possible. It actually does happen. We can all think of our favourite examples in fiction – times in *Remembrance of Things Past*, maybe Aschenbach in *Death in Venice*. But more than these cases in literature, self-deception happens in everyday life. Every time we say something like, "He knows that he won't pass his exams if he carries on like that, and still he's so confident," we attribute self-deception. If we are honest, we will probably all admit that we have done it at some time. But how does this paradoxical state happen, how can someone know something and not know it at the same time?

An explanation may be found in Freud and psychoanalytic theory. Here we have the idea of the conscious and *unconscious* parts of the mind. Something may be believed consciously and its opposite suppressed in the unconscious, and hence it would be quite correct to say that someone knows something and doesn't know it at the same time. Using the example above, maybe he thinks, consciously, that he will pass the exam and has also suppressed, in his unconscious, that painful fact that if he parties every night he won't.

But how does something get into the unconscious? There must be some part of the mind, call it the *censor*, that decides whether some truth ought to be acknowledged by the conscious mind or – if it is too unpleasant – should be suppressed and put into the unconscious. But this reply, as Sartre and others have noted, does not solve the paradox of self-deception but simply relocates it: if the censor is able to make decisions then it is, presumably, part of the conscious mind. And so the censor must know, and at the same time want to believe, the opposite, and this is simply a restatement of the original problem.

Sartre's own response to the problem of self-deception (or as he calls it *bad faith*) is that "Bad faith does not hold the norms and criteria of truth as they are accepted by the critical thought of good faith,"

(*Being and Nothingness*, Chapter 2) and so the contradiction involved in self-deception doesn't arise. This is basically to hold that consciousness has a logic of its own and this answer is not appealing to those of us who think that there can be only one logic – whatever that logic may turn out to be.

Perhaps an answer may lie in the fact that we have limited cognitive capacities. We are subjected to such a large amount of information that we have developed a pair of contradictory beliefs but *simply not noticed one of them.* This is not to say that it is hidden in our unconscious or that our consciousness has a strange logic but that we are not aware that we have such a belief and so cannot see that there is any such contradiction. Such a response is acceptable if the idea of having a belief that one has not noticed is coherent.

A final reply may be that there is in fact no real problem with self-deception. To take an analogy: If I teach you how to play backgammon then I know something that you don't – the rules of backgammon, for example, But then how do I manage to teach myself something: do I have to know something and simultaneously not know it? There is no "Paradox of Self-Teaching" so why should there by a Paradox of Self-Deception?

The true meaning of the dome

Simon Walter

The news that a corporation, headed by an eminent family practising the Hindu faith, had generously stepped forward at the last moment to sponsor the previously neglected *Spiritual Level* of the Millennium Dome, seemed to pose something of a dilemma for the embattled committee overseeing the project. Already agitated by criticism from distinguished members of the Anglican and Catholic churches, who were unhappy that Jesus had been demoted from the role of host to that of uninvited guest at his own birthday party, this gesture made the space allotted to the *metaphysical* dimension of modern life one the most controversial aspects of the exhibition. The churchmen were upset that not only was the Christian heritage of Europe being quietly forsaken but also that faith, which constituted the primary manifestation of cultural identity and conflict during the epoch being celebrated, was consequently being presented as little more than a *life-style* option. It was no longer considered the *essence* of one's sense of one's self, they complained, merely an accidental quality, like baldness. As such the life of the spirit was consigned a place, but it had no more importance than the zones reserved for Science, Technology, Work and Sport. The revered contents of the Dome now came to resemble a leisure industry trade fair.

Despite these polite protestations, Mr Mandleson, the chair of the committee, had no hesitation in accepting the unexpected bounty. Being an astute politician and a man acutely sensitive to the ebb and flow of public opinion, he knew that in the circumstances any spirituality is better than none at all even if it was not exactly what the clergy had in mind. On deeper reflection and given the esteem in which Occidental religion in general and Christianity in particular is held – somewhere between commonplace scepticism and downright animosity – the Oriental alternative must have seemed a god-send. In fact what could be a more appropriate expression of the spirit of the age. For the tribute from the Hindi community confirmed Britain's status as a truly multi-cultural commonwealth. It also blessed Mr Blair's electoral covenant with the people which declared us all to be *stakeholders* in society irrespective of creed. Better still, this eastern promise was uncannily congruent with the exotic rhetoric that the cabinet had been favouring recently in their attempt to disseminate the *Big Idea* that would distinguish them from their predecessors in government. They called it "The Third Way."

"The Third Way" seems to be a kind of Buddhist economics, with deliberate echoes of beatitude and self-realisation, that treads the narrow way between unbridled capitalism and social justice, a skilful piece of political jargon set to becalm the antagonism betwixt god and mammon. In a number of speeches and articles, Mr Blair affirmed the rights and potential of the individual as the ground of free enterprise while stressing the obligation of the state, through proper management, to ensure equality of opportunity and happiness. As *virtue* is in most forms of Buddhism a question of the flourishing of the individual, compared with the self-abnegation of Christianity, there seems to be no apparent contradiction between enlightenment and worldly success. However, in that Nirvana, the highest mode of existence for the Buddhist, can only be achieved in the state of the absence of desire, one imagines that this may not be the ideal way to stimulate an economy founded on the consumption of commodities. A rather more pertinent model for New Labour's social policy might be Aristotle's self-improvement handbook, *The Nicomachean Ethics*. There is much more common ground here. For instance the bliss of relinquishing the pursuit of satisfaction is repudiated by Aristotle's advocacy of the productive harnessing of the appetites. The "Golden Mean", between excessive indulgence and life denying abstinence, was itself the *third way* to achieve *dikaiosune*, moral or social justice, against the prevailing opinion that felicity either resided with the *pleasure seekers* or could be imposed, as Plato dreamed it could be, by an ascetic and authoritarian state. Aristotle maintained that *dikaiosune* begins with the individuals conduct and not with an allegiance to some abstract ideology emanating from a ruling elite. Furthermore, wealth, beauty and a strong constitution are the prerequisites of good character for Aristotle, a claim that Mr Blair might not openly acknowledge but one his courting of the rich and fashionable nevertheless implies. Yet, most of all, Aristotle argued that human beings were ostensibly political animals and as such a truly virtuous character would be consistently honourable in both their private and public behaviour. Plato, too, could not accept what later thinkers with liberal convictions would call the distinction between *self-regarding* and *other-regarding* actions. From this perspective it would seem that in practice Mr Blair's philosophy is really, beneath the surface, distinctly Grecian in hue. One has only to recall the recent resignation of Mr Davies, the Welsh secretary, in mysterious circumstances, to understand the importance the cabinet places on upholding the dignity of public office.

It is in this turn towards the Greeks, so to speak, that Mr Blair most radically deviates from the agenda of his antecedents in government. For it seems that the Tory party's *hubris* was not a result of polity but rather the consequence of turning a blind eye to its members' extra-curricular activities. The distinction between private and public morality is one that stretches as far back as the late 17th Century. A good example of this tradition of thinking might be Locke's *Letter Concerning Toleration* where the author argues that the public magistrate has no business interfering with the demands of private conscience. With the advent of Mrs Thatcher's government this honourable tradition became perverted. The liberal became libertarian. There is a tale, maybe apocryphal, that Mr

Joseph, the party chairman, made Mandeville's *Fable of the Bees*, required reading for all prospective Conservative parliamentary candidates. This was the satire that caused a sensation in 18th Century London by conflating economics with an abject conception of *human nature*, a philosophy expressed in the neat maxim, "Private vices, public virtues". These ideas found their modern equivalent in the character of Gordon Gekko from the film *Wall Street*. When he announced that "Greed is good", he explicitly rejected virtue, or what Aristotle called self-discipline, as contrary to the present requirements of society. The sentimental belief in the adherence to prescribed imperatives was made mockery of by a public that seemed to prosper through vicious conduct. The result of this indulgence was a decade of convulsion and violence in which very few enjoyed sustained fortune and most suffered one way or another.

For Popper, the sanctity of a private realm beyond the intrusive reach of the state was the prerequisite of a liberal and open society. The only alternative to this article of faith was a despotic tradition of political thinking that led from Plato to Stalin. After the experience of monetarism and the implicit moral values that endorsed it, Mr Blair is willing to relinquish the presuppositions of civic life in this country by turning privacy into a matter for public concern. This is the proper significance of the Millennium Dome. With its zones encompassing mind, body and spirit, all possible human knowledge is contained within its temporary structure. By visiting this site in Greenwhich we may come to comprehend the nature of modern existence. For like the transcendental categories of the understanding that synthesise intuitions in the Kantian model of consciousness, the endeavour to classify experience is necessary if we are to make sense of a world constantly in flux. Adorno once remarked that Kant's categories were more a reflection of the fragmentation of consciousness brought about by the specialisation and division of labour in modern industrial society than a true and eternal representation of the mind. At the end of the period of intense industrialisation, the Dome could be seen as another model of the conditions of possibility for experience. The beliefs and values it underwrites are ultimately derived from the social conditions of our time and as such it makes all aspects of *mental life* part of the public domain by placing them on show as a kind of paradigm worthy of imitation. Singular, unique private experience is no longer possible because the content of the Dome has already prescribed the limits of cognition. In this way all opposition and private rebellion against the public agenda is made to seem irrelevant. In other words, the Dome is, in fact, an idealised facsimile of Tony's mind. Like the Cartesian conceit that is the premise of the film "They Saved Hitler's Brain", it is a vision made concrete of an intellect transcending temporal confinements. However, the irony, of course, is that it is not being built to last.

Burning questions

Has anyone ever got rich through philosophy?

Cheryl O'Donoghue

My knowledge of past philosophers' financial situations is limited, although the contemporary author Jostein Gaarder could be said to have made millions from the subject. Of course, one can argue that Mr Gaarder is not actually a practising philosopher but a philisophical historian, reproducing the complex issues of the subject in a more simplified tome of 500 pages in the book *Sophie's World*.

W G Stewart

This reminds me of Aristotle's story of regarding Thales of Miletus, who had been made fun of because his profession as a philosopher kept him in poverty. Eventually Thales decided to demonstrate the practical value of his knowledge. On discovering in winter, through various observations, that the olive crop in the summer would be heavier than usual, Thales bought up all the olive presses in Miletus and Chios (at a low price). When the bumper summer crop was harvested, demand for the presses was high and the philosopher was able to charge a very high price as the sole supplier of the presses. Aristotle concluded, "a philosopher, when he likes, can easily become rich – but his ambition is of another sort."

John Lipczynski

The Chilean Minister of Finance under Allende, Fernando Flores, got his philosophy PhD at UC Berkeley under John Searle and Hubert Dreyfus after Allende's assassination and used what he had learned about classes of speech acts and the limitations of computers to create business facilitation software that made him rich. He's now the CEO of Business Design Associates (and many hope he'll run for President in Chile). He has a book on the subject (with Terry Winograd), *Understanding Computers and Cognition: A New Foundation for Design* (Ablex, 1986) and an excellent new book (with Charles Spinosa and Herbert Dreyfuss) called *Disclosing Worlds: Entrepreneurship, Democratic Action, and the Cultivation of Solidarity* (MIT, 1997)

Iain D. Thomson

Paradoxes
8: Conclusions
Francis Moorcroft

A thought may have occurred to the reader of this series that there may be some one, single problem that generates paradoxes, and if this could be identified then all the paradoxes could be solved in one go. Sorry, but this doesn't seem to be so: the paradoxes cover a very wide range of phenomena. It may be worth attempting to classify the paradoxes given so far to see what these phenomena are.

Paradoxes of self-reference

Under this heading comes the Liar ("This sentence is false"), Russell ("The set of all sets which do not belong to themselves"), Prediction ("No-one knows this proposition") and Self-deception ("She is deceiving herself"). All of these paradoxes have a common form: the paradoxical statements somehow refer to themselves. – *"This* sentence is false". "The set of all sets that do not belong to *themselves".* We saw that the problem was not simply one of self-reference as there are many examples of self-reference which are harmless and not at all paradoxical. To give an example: a bumper sticker may read: "If you can read this then you are riving too close". A driver who reads this should not get into philosophical perplexity – they should simply allow a greater distance between themselves and the car in front.

Apart from self-reference, these paradoxes seem to share little in common. The mathematician F P Ramsey divided paradoxes into two groups: *logical* paradoxes, such as Russell's, which involve only logical or mathematical notions such as "set" and "member of" and *semantic* paradoxes, such as the Liar, which involve notions such as truth and meaning. It may well be that these two different kinds of paradox require two very different kinds of treatments.

Also, it is not clear that a treatment of the Liar will help us to understand what goes wrong in the Paradox prediction, or lead us to a greater insight into how self-deception is possible. So even the self-referential paradoxes do not present a homogenous whole, but a diverse range of problems.

Paradoxes of infinity

The Pardoxes af Zeno, which attempt to demonstrate that motion is impossible ("A runner can never start a race", "A moving arrow is always at rest"), work by giving a line of argument, repeating it, then adding "and so on". The Racecourse, for example, is as follows: Before a runner can complete the whole course, they have to complete half the course;

before they can complete half the course they have to complete a quarter; and so on. The argument is intended to establish that the runner can never start the race, having had to do an infinite amount of things before they can even move. The argument seem reasonable, it appeals to a common sense idea of infinity: there is no smallest number, for any given number, there will always be one smaller, namely half of it. Similarly, there is n greatest number. We have to believe in infinity – mathematics wouldn't work without it (or, at best, would be pretty trivial).

The Paradoxes of Zeno clearly have a different form to the self-referential paradoxes above and so must form a different family and therefore require different techniques to be defused.

The Sorites

Here we have a third set of paradoxes. We start from the premises: *one stone is not a heap of stones* and *adding one stone to what is not a heap of stones cannot make a heap*. After a finite number of steps we arrive at the conclusion *ten thousand stones is not a heap of stones*. It is important to notice that it is a finite number of steps, as this clearly distinguishes the Sorites from the paradoxes of infinity. We also have no hint of self-reference. So we have a third set of paradoxes.

The paradoxes chosen in this series, and the classification above, are not intended to be an exhaustive survey of the field; they are merely illustrative of the guises that paradoxes take.

And now for my final remark. The reader may now feel they are due an answer to the question, "So what are the solutions to the paradoxes?" or at least, in view of the above remarks, "what is the solution to the Liar/Russell/Self-deception/Zeno?" And my reply, which some may find outrageous at this late stage, is "I don't have one". Before anger or despair sets in, I will qualify this.

I am not saying that I think there are solutions to paradoxes but I don't know which are correct; or that I have a solution but I'm not telling. I am making the stronger claim that *paradoxes don't have solutions*. This isn't because we're not clever enough to find them but because paradoxes are not the sorts of things that have solutions. Puzzles and problems have solutions but paradoxes are an entirely different sort of thing. Paradoxes start from common sense intuitive notions about such things as truth, sets, prediction, deception and heaps, and show that the common sense notion is faulty. And so we are led to think more deeply about these things to try to find out just where our common sense went wrong. Because we started with intuitive notions, the new ones we arrive at will be non-intuitive. We must make accommodations: paradoxes are not so much to be solved as to be *lived with*. There will of course be constant tension, but then such things are the stuff philosophy is made of.

Socrates in London

Leslie Stevenson

"PING-PONG" went "Thrasher" McCuss's computer, announcing his ninth e-mail message that morning. Nursing a phone on his shoulder as he spoke to his boss, he called up the text on screen. It was very short:

Can you meet 50 crates arriving Heathrow this afternoon?

"Are we expecting a delivery today?" Thrasher asked.
'Not that I know of. Who's the message from?"
"Let's see - it says:

AOTTA. co. athens.gr

"Does that mean anything to you?"
"Never heard of them. But we've done good business through Greece before, so there might be something in it for us. Look, I've gotta go meet those Arabs right now. Check this one out, will you?"
Thrasher, who had earned his nickname for his speed at computers and at making sales, was on to the Internet within seconds, searching for information on AOTTA. What came up was:

Almost Omniscient Time Travel Agency;
first registered: Athens, Greece.

"That's original", he thought, "people in our trade usually work under blander names". He decided to e-mail them back for clarification, without asking "crates of what?" - because you never know who might be tapping into the electronic traffic. So he typed in:

Re: 50 crates arriving Heathrow today.
Please clarify, and quote order number.

After another half hour, an e-mail reply pingged back, reading:-
"Our research department has established that your wife Meinou is a descendant of our client Socrates, and since he has expressed a wish to meet his family, we have arranged for him to fly to Heathrow today (14.10, Terrminal 3). We are sure you will understand."
Thrasher was used to cryptic messages in his business, but this was even more weird than usual. Presumably it was a cover for something important. His wife's name was indeed Meinou (she was Greek) – but

93

how did they know that? And who was this "Socrates"? Thrasher brought the original message back up on screen, and he now realized he had mis-read a capital "S" as a "5".

He decided to call Meinou and see if she knew anything about all this.

"How nice to have your attention in the daytime," she said, with heavy irony, "but you've chosen a bad time, I'm just off to my exercise class."

"OK, OK, just tell me quickly, have you ever heard of someone called 'Socrates'?" (Thrasher pronounced it to rhyme with "slow-crates") "He's supposed to be a relative of yours."

"Doesn't mean anything to me. Spell it."

"S-O-C-R-A-T-E-S".

"Oh, *Socrates*, you ignoramus! That was the name of a famous philosopher in ancient Athens. But I don't have any relatives with that name – it's hardly used in Greece now. What's all this about, anyway?"

"I got this strange e-mail asking me to meet someone called Socrates at Heathrow today."

"Well, you'd better go and talk to this so-called philosopher then – maybe you'll learn something! But if he's one of those shifty dealers you sometimes invite around, please don't bring him home this weekend, we all need a break. I must rush now, I'll be late for my aerobics."

Thrasher concluded that the AOTTA company were using the name "Socrates" as a cover. Looking it up on the internet brought up a long scholarly article on the Athenian philosopher, which he had no time to read, even if he had wanted to. There was no-one else to ask about it – the boss was going to be tied up with their important Arab customers for the rest of the day. Thrasher decided he'd better go to Heathrow and try to meet this mysterious "Socrates". There might be big business afoot, and you can't afford to miss any chances.

* * *

A few hours later, Thrasher found himself back in his office undergoing a gentle yet disorientating interrogation. "Socrates" was a grey-haired but vigorous man with a huge nose, and prominent eyes that managed to penetrate and twinkle at the same time. He was dressed in a sort of white robe like those the Arabs wear, but on closer inspection more like a Roman toga. He spoke English with an accent like nothing Thrasher had ever heard before, yet he was perfectly intelligible. There had been a spot of bother with Immigration at Heathrow. It seemed that he didn't have a normal Greek passport, only some sort of "time-travel" document which the authorities did not recognise. But when he told them he was expecting to meet Mr. McCuss, Deputy Director of Armchair Securities, they ran that through their computer, called in Thrasher from the waiting area to vouch for it, and Socrates was admitted to the U.K. on a temporary visa.

In the car, Socrates said that his extremely efficient travel company had established that Meinou was his nearest living relative, and had even found out her husband's e-mail address for business. "Thus I am come to Britain, a country I never knew, to meet people who did not exist in my own time", he said mysteriously. Thrasher had some experience with the devious ways of clients in his trade, so he played along with this unlikely story, hinting about arranging a meeting with Meinou. When they got to his office in Hounslow, and sat down over tea, he tried to find out what business this peculiar client was interested in doing.

"Well, now that you're here, what can I do for you? Perhaps you'd like to see some displays of what we have to offer?"

"Certainly, I'd be very interested to know what you do – and why you do it: I'm always willing to learn," replied Socrates.

"Well, we deal in a wide range of things – we have small arms, landmines, and rocket launchers immediately available, and we have contacts for some of the heavier stuff, if you're interested."

"Where I come from, we don't have these words. You will have to explain to me, for example, what a landmine is."

Thrasher wondered what guile lay behind this profession of ignorance – or perhaps his client was genuinely unsure of the English words for what he wanted. Thrasher brought up a textbook definition on screen:

> A landmine is a box containing high explosive, with a sensitive device such that when anyone treads on it, it blows up . Large numbers of landmines hidden in an area provide an economical and effective screen against penetration by infantry or tanks.

and he followed this up with a five-minute video demonstration of landmines being laid, and subsequently exploded.

"So," said Thrasher, "if that's what you're interested in, you've come to the right place. We do a wide variety of models, at very competitive prices. The cheapest is the JT509, weighing in at 5 kg - then there's the AK962, and ..."

"Forgive me for interrupting you – I see that you are a keen salesman," said Socrates, "but am I to understand that a landmine kills whoever treads on it?"

'Well, it doesn't always kill outright, but it usually does enough damage to put a soldier out of action, and that's what counts, doesn't it?"

"But it will do this damage to anyone who steps on it?"

"Yes, of course."

"So if these devices are laid in the ground in large numbers and left there, surely there are injuries to non-combatants, to children, and to animals?"

"Yes, unless precautions are taken, like recording the placings, fencing off the minefields, and removing the mines when no longer needed."

"And how often are such precautions taken?"

"I don't know. The TV news show the occasional sad picture of people who've lost limbs. But that's not my business."

"But you are selling these things? This is how you earn your living? Perhaps you are getting rich – something must pay for all these machines which I see on your desks here?"

"Sure, I'm selling weapons. But I'm not responsible for how they're used – that's up to the buyers. And I'm not exactly rich. This firm's making a profit – so far, and I can pay my mortgage. But it's a very competitive market. We have to work like mad to stay in business."

To his own surprise, Thrasher found himself drawn into this unusually frank discussion. Before he could reflect on what was going on, he found himself in deeper water, as Socrates' insistent questions continued:

"So you think it is right to sell these devices which so often kill and injure non-combatants?"

"It's perfectly legal, as long as we avoid exporting direct to the countries on the government's blacklist."

"That wasn't what I asked. Do you think it is *right* ?"

"Well it's in the interests of our company, and it's in my self-interest too – that's how I support my family. Judging from the way the government likes to encourage exports, it's in the national interest too."

"So on your view, whatever is in your self-interest is right?"

"I reckon so. It's every man for hinself in this world."

"So whatever is in anyone's self-interest is right for him or her?"

"Sure."

"Are you so sure that you *know* what's in your own self-interest?"

"Surely I'm the best judge of that?"

"Well, this may seem a strange question, but what counts as your *self* ?"

"What on earth do you mean by that?"

"I mean that when you judge the rightness of an action by its advantage to yourself, do you consider yourself as one individual human being, distinct from all others – including your wife, your children, your extended family?"

Thrasher considered this for a moment. Then he remembered something of a TV programme about selfish genes recently, and it occurred to him to say (and, indeed, he thought it rather clever):

"Well, I guess I judge by the advantage *primarily* to myself, but also to people I'm related to, in proportion to the genes I share with them."
"Where does that leave your wife – you don't share genes with *her*?"
"Well, I'm very fond of her, despite our occasional tiffs. Maybe it's because she's the mother of my son, who does carry my genes, and he's still very dependent on her."
"What about the other members of your company? – I presume you don't share genes with them. Don't you care about them?"
"Well, I get along well enough with them, but it's only a business relationship. People leave firms, or get fired, all the time. There's no deeper attachment – you're a fool if there is."
"And you mentioned the national interest a moment ago – how does that relate to your self-interest?"
"I'm not sure I care very much about that, either. Of course, we have to take account of the laws and regulations that hold in the UK – though in this trade we're quite good at finding ways round them. Politicians make noises about the national interest, but it's hardly my concern. If our company decided to relocate in another country, I wouldn't shed any tears, if the conditions were right."
"So for you, what is right is what is to your own advantage (and to the advantage of your genes). But how do you judge that? You have to plan ahead, to be rational. How can you know what is in your self-interest in the longer term?"
"One has to make judgments as best one can. In business we take calculated risks, trying to cover ourselves against losses, while hoping to make substantial profits. I guess the same applies in the rest of life. Don't you know the saying: 'Probability is the guide of life'?"
Thrasher had mixed feelings about the direction this conversation had taken. It didn't seem to be leading towards business, but he had quite enjoyed exercising his intelligence to bat back answers. But then Socrates' questioning took an even more personal turn:
"So when you got married, and promised to stay with your wife 'until death do us part', you did not really mean what you said. Rather, the continuation of your commitment to her is conditional on your estimate of the probability of her good behaviour, where that means behaviour that is to your advantage?"
"That's a rather crude way of putting it. Things are usually quite good between us, and I hope they go on that way. But a lot of couples split up these days, and I suppose when a relationship breaks down, it's rational to get out of it."
"Could it be that a prevaling attitude of computing self-interest makes breakdowns more likely?"
'I don't know. I'm not a psychologist."
"What about your children? Is your commitment to them similarly conditional on good behaviour?"

"Actually, we've only got one son, so far. And his behaviour is some-times atrocious. There are times when I could gladly do without him."

"But you don't really want to be without him, do you? What if someone else volunteered to take him over?"

"That'll be the day!"

"Imagine that you'd never see him again. And that you had no more children."

Thrasher shifted in his chair, and said, after a moment's thought, "I suppose there would be something missing."

"And when he's older, what will you tell him about your business?"

"I hope I can tell him how successful I've been, and how I've been able to buy him the things he wants."

"Would it be good for him to get everything he wants? And what will you say when he asks how you made your money? Will you tell him about the people who've been injured or killed by landmines?"

"Like I said, that's not my business."

"But your business *is* selling them. If nobody sold them, they wouldn't get used, would they?"

"If I didn't sell them, someone else would, so it makes no differ-ence."

"Suppose you were a policeman in a country where torture was routine. If you refused to torture prisoners, someone else certainly would. Would that make it all right for you to do it?"

"That's a different case. I'm not torturing anyone."

"But you are providing the means by which people are maimed. Surely there are other ways for you to make a living? Even if you make a fortune, will you be able to feel content with yourself at the end of your life?"

Thrasher McCuss's patience gave out. He'd been feeling increas-ingly uncomfortable as this dialogue continued, and he now wondered how he had let himself in for it, and why he had let it go on so long. He burst out:

"Look, Mr. Socrates, I don't know what game you're playing. I thought you came here to *buy* , but this is a pretty strange way of going about it. If you're not interested in doing business with us, then I've got other things to do with my time. As I said, it's a very competitive market."

Socrates said, "My business is to understand, and help others un-derstand."

Just then, the phone rang. Thrasher picked it up, and Socrates heard him say:

"Oh hello, Dave. ... Is that the time? I've been talking to a client here. ... Sure, I remember. OK, see you there in an hour or so."

He put the receiver down and stared at his visitor.

"Mr. Socrates, I have a dinner date with some colleagues. Is there any other business you have to do in London?"

"My hope was to meet your wife, who, I am reliably informed, is a descendant of mine."

Thrasher had forgotten about that unlikely story.

"And haven't you made any other arrangements? Have you a hotel?"

"I was relying on the hospitality of my family." Socrates said this with such a smile that even Thrasher was disarmed, and found himself saying:

"Well, you'd better come and meet my friends, and then we'll see what we can sort out for you."

* * *

Two hours later Thrasher and Socrates were sitting in a club in Soho called "The Naked Truth". Thrasher had introduced Socrates – whom he still described as 'his client', despite the strange afternoon dialogue – to his friends, Dave from the Department of Trade and Industry, and Quentin from the Foreign Office. The latter reminisced about how he had studied the philosophy of Socrates when he was at Oxford, and joked about how pleased he was to meet the philosopher himself. Socrates smiled benignly. Thrasher remarked that they'd been having an ethical discussion in his office. Dave and Quentin roared with laughter:

"What? You, Thrasher, of all people, taking lessons in ethics? That's rich!"

Thrasher said, only half in jest, "Well, he did make me think."

Socrates laughed with them, and then studied the menu with interest. He needed to have some of the words explained to him, but when the food came he displayed a lusty appetite for it – and for the wine. He downed the latter at a greater rate than the others, yet without displaying any symptoms other than a somewhat greater intensity in those impressive eyes.

After the plates were cleared away, and as they opened another bottle, a young lady in a sequinned body-hugging outfit sidled up to their table, and said, in a synthetic voice:

"Good evening, gentlemen. My name is Phoebe. I hope you've enjoyed your meal?"

"Yes, thank you, Phoebe", said Dave, "and what can you offer us tonight?"

"Well", she simpered, "I do a belly-dance for a mere tenner, or the topless treat at £20, or the full Phoebe for £30 – plus of course any gratuities you would like to add as special appreciation."

"What is she talking about?" asked Socrates.

"She will dance for us," said Thrasher. "Erotically", he added.

"In my time it was boys who did that sort of thing," said Socrates, "women were kept strictly in the home. I am learning."

"Mr. Socrates," said Quentin, who thought he knew how to entertain Middle Eastern clients, "please allow me to treat you to the full Phoebe." So saying he produced three crisp notes from his wallet. Phoebe pushed a shapely thigh through a slit in her dress, and Quentin deftly slipped them into a strategically-placed garter. Rhythmic music began to emanate from the walls around their table, and she slipped into an apparently well-practised routine.

The centre of her outfit split, revealing a tanned abdomen which started to writhe in time to the beat. Socrates soon found himself treated to the sight of a belly-button gyrating lasciviously within a few inches of his face. His smile broadened. After Phoebe had given the other three men a turn of this display, she began to peel off her outer costume. Underneath she wore very little – just some black lace and stringy stuff which ostentatiously drew attention to what it barely concealed. Trying to follow the rhythms of the music, she proceeded to toy with the upper sections of her black apparatus, and after various teasing contortions, one nipple, then two, were wobbling near Socrates' lips (which were themselves somewhat large and fleshy). His smile faded somewhat. After cavorting round the table, to the applause of Thrasher, Quentin and Dave, she started untwisting the remaining wisps of material.

At this point, Socrates' eyes flashed, and he suddenly said:

"Phoebe, why are you doing this?"

Taken aback, she said "Aren't you enjoying it?"

"Well it arouses appetite, even in a man of my age – though I must say I find it more erotic when something is left to the imagination. But my reason tells me you are not really doing it to please me – there is surely no question of satisfying appetite here. In fact, isn't it rather like placing a delicious-smelling dish before a hungry person, and then whisking it away – which is not actually very pleasing!"

"Well, the rule of the house is: no touching."

"So I inferred. So there's nothing personal about this, there's no emotion, no question of love – or even liking or friendship. You don't get to know the people here, do you?"

Phoebe had continued to go through some of her motions as this conversation proceeded, but by now she was quite put off her rhythm, and left off fingering her remaining wisps of clothing.

"Actually we're not supposed to talk to the customers, except for the initial chat-up."

"So you're expected to bare your body, but baring the soul is forbidden?"

"I guess so. I don't think I'd want to bare my soul to the sort of people who come here, anyway. I'm only doing this for the money."

"Just as I thought. And why do you need the money so much?"

"I'm studying at university, and my parents don't support me, so I've got to pay my fees somehow."

"What are you studying, may I ask?"

"Philosophy," she admitted, with an embarrassed smile.

"Ah, philo-sophia: the love of wisdom," Socrates pronounced, with emphasis.

Before either of them could say more, the music was switched off, and three men in dinner suits approached the table, two of them of formidable size.

"What's going on here?" said the smallest, who was the manager of the club.

"He was only having a philosophical dialogue with her," said Thrasher.

"Oh yeah, that's what they all say," leered the larger of the heavy men.

"Oh hallo there Quentin, nice to see you here again," said the manager, "but you must explain the rules to your guests: no touching."

Phoebe interjected, "He only talked to me. In fact, he touched my mind, not my body. I'm not sure I want to do this any more."

"Oh really? Well, that's your privilege, darling. There's plenty more out there to take your place."

Phoebe picked up her discarded clothing, and disappeared.

Jones indicated Socrates to his assistants: "This fellow's corrupting my young dancers. See him out, will you?"

Ugly smiles on two large faces indicated a delight in the performance of their ejaculatory role. Socrates found himself lifted abruptly to his feet, and propelled rapidly through the room. At the back door of "The Naked Truth" two feet were expertly applied to his backside, and his face hit the street with force. When Thrasher caught up with him, he said "I'd better take you home."

* * *

The next morning Thrasher woke up beside Meinou, recollecting the events of the previous afternoon and evening. As she moved towards consciousness he wondered how to tell her there was a visiting Greek of mysterious purpose sleeping on the sofa in the living room. Then he remembered Socrates' claim to family membership, and thought that might be a useful cover-story. So after a tentative good morning kiss, he said, "There's someone downstairs who claims to be your long-lost relative."

"Go on, pull the other leg! Is this another of your tedious clients? I *told* you not to bring anyone home."

"This one's different. Don't you remember? We talked about him on the phone. He's called 'Socrates'. He has a charming way of asking difficult questions."

"We have enough difficult questions in this house already. I *asked* you to give me a break this weekend."

"He really is something else. Meet him anyway, and see what you think."

Meinou went downstairs in a foul mood. In the living room of 27 Brickhill Gardens, NW6, lay a figure with a bushy beard, tousled hair and a bloodied nose, wrapped in a crumpled sheet – or was it a toga? Hearing their entry, he opened his eyes and struggled to his feet. Thrasher introduced him as "Mr. Socrates, from Athens".

Socrates said, "Meinou, I see something Greek in your eyes straight away. I am have been told that you are my nearest living descendant. I am come to inquire if virtue is still being taught in your generation."

Meinou had never heard such a speech before, and suspected that either this fellow was crazy, or she was the victim of a distinctly unfunny joke. She replied tartly:

"I know of no relative by your name. What generation would you be, then?"

"By my estimate, about a hundred generations ago."

This was getting crazier. Yet there was something about the eyes and demeanour of this old man that commanded respect. She looked at him in puzzled silence. Just then her son Jason came running in, and shouted "Dad, can you take me to the football this afternoon?"

Thrasher groaned slightly, and said, "We haven't decided yet."

"So this is the hundred and first generation?" said Socrates.

"This is Jason," said Thrasher.

Over breakfast, which she felt constrained to offer, Meinou suddenly had an idea: "Since you're here, Mr. Socrates, why don't you play with Jason for a bit, while his Dad and I get on with the chores we have to do today?" To Thrasher she said, sharply:

"Come on, you cut the grass while I do the shopping."

Socrates said with a smile, "I see that the woman still wants to rule the man within the household. I had similar troubles myself."

On returning from the supermarket Meinou came in to see what was going on. Jason was upstairs in his room playing a computer game, and Socrates was sitting on the sofa, apparently lost in thought.

"Well, what do you make of the hundred and first generation?" said Meinou, playing along with their visitor's joke or delusion.

"He showed me his favourite programmes on this thing you call a TV, and some of the games he plays on that other screen you call a computer. And he played me some of that extremely noisy music he seems to like – what does it do to the soul, I wonder? In between we had quite a rational conversation for a while. I even got him to do a bit of geometry with me – we proved a theorem, between the two of us."

"Amazing! We never manage anything like that with him."

"He has some innate talent. But what he most wants to do is to watch those screens."

"I know. He'll spend most of his time that way, if we let him."

"And what is he watching? Some of it is violent, some of it just seems silly. He is looking at mere shadows, or images – or images of images. It's like spending your life in a cave, out ot touch with reality."

"What annoys *me* most is the advertisments. They're put on in the middle of children's programmes, of course, and then of course Jason wants to get all those things he sees pictures of."

"Who decides what images are put before the young? Whoever they are, they have immense power, if the same things are going into every home."

"Well, there are the large television companies, and of course there are the advertisers who want to sell their products,"

"Ah, the power of images! And of money! People are so easily influenced. I still wonder how can virtue ever be taught?"

"Yes, it worries me. One feels so helpless against all these influences."

"But not completely powerless, surely? The state has great power, and so have the rich, but they are not omnipotent. Individual people still have minds, and can make choices."

Meinou suddenly felt tears forming in her eyes, and she said "Socrates, I'm beginning to believe..."

At that moment there was a loud knock on the front door. Two men in suits stood there. One held up a plastic card and said, "Immigration department. Is there a Mr. S. O. Crates here?"

For a few seconds Meinou was nonplussed, then she said "Perhaps you mean Socrates? We have a visitor of that name."

"That'll be him," said the other man. "We need to see him – right now."

On finding him in the living room, the first man said "Are you Mr. S. O. Crates, otherwise known as Socrates, of Athens, Greece?"

Socrates said, "I am he."

"The Home Secretary has determined that your presence in the United Kingdom is not conducive to the public good. I must therefore require you to come with me to Heathrow for deportation. You have ten minutes to pack your bags."

"I have no bags," said Socrates, "I am ready now."

* * *

That was the last that Thrasher and Meinou saw of Socrates. On Monday, Thrasher e-mailed AOTTA to ask about him. The reply came:

Socrates was a Greek philosopher who saw himself as having a duty to make people think about the purpose of their actions and lives. He was found guilty by the Athenians of subverting the state religion and corrupting the young. He was condemned to death by drinking hemlock in 399 B.C.

This company has now gone out of business, and no further messages to this address will be answered.

Sci Phi

4: Immaterial minds

Mathew Iredale

...the human mind can be perceived clearly and distinctly as a substance which is distinct from a corporeal substance.

Rene Descartes

If science has influenced one area of philosophy more than any other then that area must be the philosophy of mind. And if there is one philosophical theory that science appears to have comprehensively refuted then it must be the theory of mind known as mind-brain dualism (or Cartesian dualism, as it is sometimes called, after its most famous exponent, Rene Descartes). While there continues to be disagreement between philosophers over the exact nature of consciousness, it is fair to say that there is almost universal agreement that consciousness, whatever it is, is purely a product of physical processes.

The scientific evidence against dualism appears to be sound. Not only is there very strong evidence from the neurosciences that normal brain function alone is sufficient to enable consciousness, making a separate mind redundant, it has also been argued that mind-brain dualism would violate one of the conservation laws of physics – the law of conservation of energy. This law requires that the total energy in a closed physical system is constant. But if the non-physical mind controls the physical brain then surely energy of some sort must pass from the non-physical realm to the physical, which would mean that energy in the physical realm would not be constant, thus violating the law of conservation.

Such a problem merely confirms the generally held belief that dualism is a theory with little or no scientific support. However, as if to beat the materialists at their own game, it is to science that two of the supporters of dualism have turned in order to show that no such violation of the conservation laws need take place.

According to the physicist Henry Margenau, "the mind may be regarded as a field in the accepted physical sense of the term. But it is a nonmaterial field; its closest analogue is perhaps a probability field." By likening the mind to a probability field, a recognised physical phenomenon in quantum mechanics, Margenau is able to hypothesise how the mind could overcome violating conservation laws:

> In very complicated physical systems such as the brain, the
> neurons, and sense organs, whose constituents are small enough
> to be governed by probabilistic quantum laws, the physical organ
> is always poised for a multitude of possible changes, each with a

definite probability; if one change takes place that requires energy, or more or less energy than another, the intricate organism furnishes it automatically. Hence, even if the mind has anything to do with the change, that is, if there is mind-body interaction, the mind would not be called upon to furnish energy.

The question that remains, though, is exactly where these constituents are. It is one thing to postulate microscopic constituents in the brain that may be affected in the way Margenau describes, it is quite another to positively identify them.

It is at this point that we must turn to the work of the late Sir John Eccles. In his paper "Do mental events cause neural events analogously to the probability fields of quantum mechanics?" he argued that suitable microscopic sites for the action of a non-material mind are the tiny vesicles that occur at the tips of nerve cells in the brain. The numerous vesicles carry the transmitter substances that allow nerve cells to communicate with each other. Eccles argued that the emission of these vesicles is small enough to be affected by a quantum probability wave and therefore that they could also be affected by a non-material mind:

> It can be concluded that calculations on the basis of the Heisenberg uncertainty principle show that the probabilistic emission of a vesicle from the ... vesicular grid could conceivably be modified by a mental intention acting analogously to a quantal probability field.

Eccles stresses in the article that he is not suggesting that the mind actually causes the vesicular emission, but rather that the mental events merely alter the probability of a vesicular emission that is triggered by a nerve impulse. He also recognised that the order of magnitude of the effect, which is merely a change in probability of emission of a single vesicle, is far too small to modify the patterns of nerve cell activity even in small areas of the brain. However, as there are many thousands of nerve endings containing vesicles his hypothesis is that the probability field of a mental intention is widely distributed so that it not only affects one particular nerve cell, but also a multitude of other nerve cells with similar functions. If the mind can change the probability of emission of the vesicles in many thousands of nerve cells then, Eccles argued, the mind will be able to exert an influence upon the brain without any violation of conservation laws.

Eccles hoped that his research would open up "an immense field of scientific investigation both in quantum physics and in neuroscience". Although this seems somewhat optimistic, at the very least he has shown that one should not be too hasty in dismissing mind-brain dualism as unscientific nonsense, as many philosophers do. Nonsense it maybe, but not necessarily unscientific.